D1261114

MAN AS CHURCHMAN

THE WILES LECTURES

GIVEN AT THE QUEEN'S UNIVERSITY

BELFAST 1959

MAN AS CHURCHMAN

BY

NORMAN SYKES, F.B.A.

DEAN OF WINCHESTER
HONORARY FELLOW OF EMMANUEL COLLEGE
CAMBRIDGE

L'histoire de l'Église, cette série d'événements et de personnages gigantesques, qui préoccupe aujourd'hui tant d'esprits étrangers, sinon hostiles, aux convictions religieuses

MONTALEMBERT in 1847

CAMBRIDGE
AT THE UNIVERSITY PRESS
1960

PUBLISHED BY
THE SYNDICS OF THE CAMBRIDGE UNIVERSITY PRESS
Bentley House, 200 Euston Road, London, N.W. 1
American Branch: 32 East 57th Street, New York 22, N.Y.

Printed in Great Britain at the University Press, Cambridge
(Brooke Crutchley, University Printer)

ALWYNO EPISCOPO WINTON:
PRAESULI DILECTO NECNON AMICO SINCERO
HOC AMICITIAE PIGNUS
DEDICAT
DISCIPULUS ET SOCIUS

CONTENTS

PREFACE

To the Trustees of the Wiles Lectures I owe the honour and privilege of their invitation to deliver these lectures in the Queen's University, Belfast in May 1959, and I should like to express to them my grateful thanks for the opportunity of lecturing on so distinguished a foundation. The terms of the Trust require the lecturer to relate the topics of his specialised researches to wider themes of general interest in his field of study; and to this end a number of scholars expert in cognate subjects are invited in order to submit him to trial by his peers in informal discussion at the end of each lecture. Fortunately for the victim, the ordeal is assuaged by the generous hospitality administered to him at all times outside the actual lectures and discussion. I am particularly grateful to Mr and Mrs Austin Boyd for their kind welcome and entertainment of my wife and myself on the evening of our arrival, to Sir Eric and Lady Ashby who gave an official reception before the first lecture, and to Professors Michael Roberts and J. C. Beckett who cared for all our waking hours from arrival to departure. A Wiles lecturer must needs carry away the liveliest recollections of the cordial reception accorded to him, both on public and private occasions, throughout his stay in Belfast.

In conformity with the terms of the Trust, I have

tried to consider various issues raised by a study of ecclesiastical history in relation to their contemporary context, with especial reference to the oecumenical tendencies amongst all Christian Churches at the present time and in prospect of the challenge of totalitarian States. I am most grateful for the criticisms and suggestions made during discussion by visiting scholars and by members of the Queen's University. Amongst the former were the Master of Peterhouse, Cambridge (Professor Herbert Butterfield), Dr S. L. Greenslade, Regius Professor of Ecclesiastical History in the University of Oxford, Dr C. W. Dugmore, Professor of Ecclesiastical History in the University of London, Dr J. M. Barkley, Professor of Ecclesiastical History in the Presbyterian College, Belfast, Dr. G. F. Nuttall, Professor of Ecclesiastical History at New College, London, Dr T. M. Parker, Fellow of University College, Oxford, Dr W. H. C. Frend, Fellow of Gonville and Caius College, Cambridge, and Dr G. F. A. Best, Fellow of Trinity Hall, Cambridge; whilst among the latter, in addition to the staff of the History Department, were Professors C. F. Carter, T. A. Sinclair, H. W. Rodgers, and also Monsignor Ryan and the Reverend Dr C. B. Daly. Although some of the topics were of a potentially controversial character, the discussions throughout were entirely constructive and eirenic and contributed much to my own edification.

I regret that these lectures went to press before the publication of Mr T. A. Roberts' *History and*

Christian Apologetic, since otherwise I should have enjoyed breaking a lance with him in respect of his rebuke of my shibboleth in speaking of 'fact plus interpretation', instead of adopting his sibboleth of 'fact plus explanation'. I am greatly indebted to the unwearying patience and perseverance of Mrs J. R. Morgan in typing my manuscript for the press. The Secretary of the Cambridge University Press and the various members of the Printer's staff have shown me their wonted kindness, just as if I had not ceased to enjoy the privilege of membership of the Syndicate.

N. S.

WINCHESTER
St Swithun's Day, 1960

CHAPTER I

CHURCH HISTORY, HISTORY AND THEOLOGY

'All learned men agree', wrote the Spanish Dominican Melchior Cano, in *De Locis Theologicis* published posthumously in 1563, 'that those theologians are altogether ignorant, in whose lucubrations history is silent. To myself indeed they seem to be no theologians, nor even of sufficient learning, to whom the events of the past are unknown. For history furnishes from its treasures many things to us, which, if we lack, both in theology and in almost every other discipline, we are frequently found insufficient and unlearned.'[1] So high an evaluation of history represented the tardy coming-of-age of a study which had hitherto enjoyed little regard. During the long millennium of the Middle Ages the scholastic theologians had deemed even ecclesiastical history of little relevance or service to their dogmatic systems. Moreover, with the advent of the Reformation in the sixteenth century, Protestant and Catholic alike considered Church history chiefly as ancillary to systematic theology. 'Les auteurs protestantes du XVIème siècle n'ont envisagé l'histoire de l'Église que comme faisant partie de la théologie; ils ne l'ont guère connue comme constituant une science séparée et indépendante.'[1] In the German universities founded as a result of the ferment of reform, as well as in the older foundations won for Lutheranism, the curriculum centred in the study of the Bible and its original tongues. History entered into their purview mainly, as with Bossuet in the following century, as a *praeparatio evangelica* and in the form of *discours sur l'histoire universelle* (to borrow Bossuet's title). At Heidelberg, for example, the professorship of history was combined with that of poetry from 1556 to 1561; whilst in the Calvinist universities at Geneva, Montpellier and Saumur likewise, the teaching of history was undertaken by philologists. Nîmes indeed was a pioneer in the establishment of a chair of history as a separate discipline, though here also universal history figured prominently in the curriculum; and not until the seventeenth century did the academic teaching of history gain recognition as an autonomous province. Moreover, although Melanchthon and his disciples had established in theory the distinction between Church history and secular history, the credit of developing ecclesiastical history as an independent study belonged largely to the universities of Strasbourg and Basle, thanks to the labours at the former of Caspar Hedio (1499–1552) and John Pappus (1549–1601) and at the latter of John Grynaeus (1540–1617). At Saumur also David Blondel (1590–1655) adorned his honorary professorship by the publication of his *De la Primauté en l'Église*, his *Apologia pro Sententia Hieronymi de*

Presbyteris et Episcopis, and his *De Joanna Papissa*. At Geneva a chair of ecclesiastical history was created especially for Jean Alphonse Turrettini in 1697, and in Scotland professorships of Church history were founded at Edinburgh in 1694, at St Andrews in 1707 and at Glasgow in 1718; whilst Aberdeen, like the English universities of Oxford and Cambridge, had to wait until the nineteenth century for a similar foundation. In the Roman Catholic universities of Fribourg and Mainz, professorships of history were established in 1572 and 1584 respectively; whilst the exclusion of history from the *Ratio Studiorum* of the Society of Jesus meant that in Ingolstadt, and other universities under their influence, the study of this subject enjoyed little attention.

Notwithstanding the slow development and belated recognition of Church history as an independent subject of academic study, the seventeenth century saw a growing interest in and emphasis on its importance as ancillary to the exploration of theological and ecclesiastical issues. 'If during the seventeenth century, history was able to penetrate the academy, it was surreptitiously, so to speak, and under cover of what is now called "positive theology"....By this means a door was opened to history and criticism....If, furthermore, it is remembered that after 1640 Catholics were compelled more and more to follow Protestants in matters of controversy into the field of antiquity, where the latter for the time being had chosen to fight, the advance made by history, concealed under the name of "positive theology", towards the middle of the seventeenth century will be easily understood.'[1] A great cloud of witnesses can be called in support of this conclusion. Antoine Godeau, bishop of Vence, in the preface to his *Histoire de l'Église*, published in 1653, declared: 'I do not intend here to argue the commonplace of the usefulness of history. Many learned authors have exhausted this subject, and I have nothing new to add....The proof of it we see in many modern writers and especially in many scholastics, who through imperfect knowledge of the history of doctrine have made mistakes which give ground to their adversaries to accuse them of ignorance or even of bad faith....Thus ecclesiastical history is absolutely essential to writers who treat of doctrine in order to avoid blunders....On the one hand the indispensable law of history, which is to tell the truth, is obligatory on the historian, and his duty is to pay heed to nothing which is to the prejudice of truth....Church history has need of this kind of enlightened and sincere criticism, and it must be confessed that without it we should be still in profound ignorance of many very useful things.'[2] In parallel vein Alexander Natalis, the French Dominican, in the preface to his *Selecta Historiae Ecclesiasticae Capita*, avowed that he reckoned a man who, though versed in scholastic questions, was only distantly acquainted with the Bible, Church history, the councils and doctrine of the Fathers, as but half a theologian; whilst he pronounced virtually useless to the Church one ignorant and unversed in these studies.[1] To Bernard Lamy indeed 'theology is simply the history of what God has revealed to men, or of what the Church has believed at all times; and for this reason church history is its principal part'.[2] To Du Pin likewise it was the glory of his century to have driven from the theological schools the barbarism hitherto prevailing, and to have substituted for scholastic subtleties a theology founded on Scripture and Tradition.[3] But perhaps the crowning testimony was that of Jean Mabillon, whose chapter 'De l'étude de l'histoire sacrée et profane', in his *Traité des Études Monastiques*, ascribed the highest value and importance to this discipline. 'This study is of much greater value than the majority of mankind supposes, and the strongest reasons exist for applying oneself to it, especially to the study of ecclesiastical history. For it is certain that without this study it is impossible to have a complete understanding of the Fathers, or of theology; and by it may be learned not only morality by examples but also the dogmas of our religion.' After citing the statements of Cano and Godeau, he adduced further contemporary testimony. 'In fine, I have understood from one of the most famous authors of this century, who from his birth had been nourished in heresy, that nothing had contributed more to disabuse him of his error than the reading of church history.'[4]

In essaying to discharge the responsibility incumbent upon a lecturer on this foundation, I propose to consider in detail some vital issues arising from this revival of interest in Church history during the sixteenth and seventeenth centuries; but first it seems necessary to examine the relationship of ecclesiastical history to other branches of that discipline and also to theology, and to ask whether certain criticisms of its nature and theme, offered by historians of other schools, affect its claim to be accepted as a truly historical exercise.

From one aspect, indeed, as Gwatkin repeatedly insisted, ecclesiastical history may be regarded as simply the spiritual side of universal history, and as such its intimate relationship with other aspects—political, constitutional and economic—is evident. From this standpoint it cannot be profitably studied without constant reference to each of these aspects, for the history of the Church is closely bound up in every age with that of the society within which *sub specie hujus saeculi* it lives and moves and has its being. Examples of this interdependence can be cited from many epochs. Thus Dr S. L. Greenslade's study of *Schism in the Early Church* has emphasised the non-theological factors affecting the doctrinal controversies of the early centuries, and Dr W. H. C. Frend's *The Donatist Church* has illustrated this with particular relation to the Donatist Schism; Dr Ulrich Stutz's survey of *Die Eigenkirche als Element des mittelalterlichgermanischen Kirchenrechtes* threw a flood of light on the protracted process by which the Proprietary Church was integrated with the law and constitution of the medieval western Church; the history of the Reformation must be set against the contemporary background of social and economic conditions, as the perennial question of *Religion and the Rise of Capitalism* testifies, and as Mr Christopher Hill's *Economic Problems of the Church from Whitgift to the Long Parliament* has demonstrated in regard to England; the influence of the ecclesiastical measures of the French Revolution and Napoleonic Empire on the Gallican Church has engaged the attention of a generation of historians from Aulard to Latreille; whilst few episodes of Church history have been more fascinatingly portrayed than the struggle of the papacy with a totalitarian regime in Professor D. A. Binchy's *Church and State in Fascist Italy*, particularly in the decade between the Lateran Treaties of 1929 and the death of Pius XI in 1939. Little complaint can be justly made indeed against contemporary ecclesiastical historians of neglect of other aspects of history, affecting the development not only of institutions, but also of doctrines of the Church. Rather Church historians might wish that secular historians and men of affairs would be at pains to inform themselves more perfectly concerning the history of Christianity and the Church. Thus in H. A. L. Fisher's *History of Europe*, his account of Christianity, making a bashful and somewhat incongruous appearance in the chapter headed 'Greece and Macedon', begins with the statement that 'we know little of the life of Jesus'; whilst the apostolic churches are described as 'democratic, universalist and egalitarian' (despite the contrary evidence of the Pauline Epistles concerning the authority exercised by the Apostles); the conciliar epoch is characterised in Gibbonian phrase as a debate on 'the nature of the Second Person of the Trinity, which few were fitted to discuss and none were able to understand'; and the astonishing statement is made that 'the parish... was the gift of Roman churchmen to Saxon England'. Again, few passages of more delicate irony can be found than that in which Professor Binchy describes the mystification of Mussolini when Cardinal Gasparri, receiving him on 11 February 1929 at the Lateran Palace for the signature of the Treaty and Concordat, 'began by making his visitor welcome in "the Holy Father's own parochial house". Mussolini bowed, obviously mystified: how was he to know that the Lateran is the pope's episcopal church? "Especially", the cardinal continued, "as today is the feast of Our Lady of Lourdes, Protectress of the Apostolic See." Mussolini bowed again. "And also the anniversary of the Pope's coronation." The Duce, feeling himself at last on firm ground, smiled broadly. "Yes," he said, "I knew that."'

Ecclesiastical history may, furthermore, claim an identity of purpose and method with other aspects of human history, not only in respect of a common subject-matter, but also in regard to the treatment and criticism of its sources. In the latter respect it knows both how to abound and how to be in want. It is a commonplace that the extant literary sources for the early centuries of the history of the Church are exiguous; and that between the Acts of the Apostles in the first century and the *Ecclesiastical History* of Eusebius in the fourth century, the Church historian has to be content with such scanty gleanings as episcopal succession lists and similar chronological data. The paucity of information for the sub-apostolic age is particularly vexing, since it embraced the period of the evolution of the incipient Church-Order of the New Testament into the monarchical episcopate of Ignatius, whilst the later epoch witnessed the development of the authority of the see of Rome; and it was round the claims of episcopacy and papacy that much of the sixteenth-century Reformation controversy was to turn. Eusebius indeed proclaimed himself 'the first to enter on the undertaking, as travellers on some desolate and untrodden way', in which 'nowhere can we find even the bare footsteps of men who have preceded us in the same path, unless it be those slight indications by which in divers ways they have left to us partial accounts of the times through which they have passed, raising their voices as a man holds up a torch from afar, calling to us from on high as from a distant watch-tower'.[1]

This paucity of information, however, is not peculiar to the ecclesiastical historian. 'If we go back to early times', wrote Sir Charles Firth of the secular historian, 'the imperfect nature of evidence is forced upon us at every moment. It is often a question of the interpretation of a single sentence or the trustworthiness of a single document. Even in dealing with better-known periods, such as the seventeenth century, the same difficulty arises. Often the really conclusive document is missing; we know that something happened; but the piece of evidence which would explain why it happened is non-existent; and the precise significance of the fact becomes a matter for inference or conjecture.... Everywhere therefore the historian is made conscious of the limitations of his own knowledge about the past and the limitations of men's possible knowledge. He feels he moves in a little circle of light, seeing as far as his little candle throws its beams; and beyond that comes darkness.'[1] In Church history, as elsewhere, with the chronological advance into the high Middle Ages and thence into modern times, the candle of the student is set upon a bushel and the circle of its radiance so extended that it gives light to all in the house.

The crux of the matter lies, however, not in the number of sources available, but in the standards of criticism governing their interpretation. Does the ecclesiastical historian adhere to the same austere methods and principles of critical scholarship as are observed in other fields of historical discipline? Or is there just ground for the repeated accusations levelled by Professor E. T. Merrill against 'an ecclesiastical temper of mind', which deflects the Church historian from the straight path of scholarly rectitude? The fourfold repetition of this charge, in an essay of twenty-seven pages 'On Materials and

Methods', rests on the suspicion that 'the professed student of early Christian history...is lamentably inclined to disregard the ordinary rules and principles of historical evidence; that he is willing for the sake of his cause to welcome as valid testimony such as he would not for a moment dream of accepting, if he were dealing with any other class of subjects; that, however competent he may otherwise be as a scholar, when he touches upon matters connected with Christian antiquities, he too frequently appears to slip, though unconsciously, from the chair of record and of judgement into that of some special advocacy; and that the whole fabric of generally accepted early Christian history is influenced in its constitution by such an erroneous spirit'.[1] The question is of primary importance for the student of ecclesiastical history, since it concerns not only the history of the Christian Church, but also the historicity of those events in the life of its Founder upon which its theological doctrines and religious beliefs are based. For, as Marc Bloch emphasised in his study of *The Historian's Craft*, 'Christianity is a religion of historians. Other religious systems have been able to found their beliefs and their rites on a mythology nearly outside human time. For sacred books, the Christians have books of history, and their liturgies commemorate, together with episodes from the terrestrial life of a God, the annals of the church and the lives of the saints. Christianity is historical in another, and perhaps even deeper, sense. The destiny of humankind, placed between the Fall and the Judgement, appears to its eyes as a long adventure, of which each life, each individual pilgrimage, is in its turn a reflection. It is in time and therefore in history, that the great drama of Sin and Redemption, the central axis of all Christian thought, is unfolded.' And again, 'Christianity...is essentially a historical religion; a religion, that is, whose prime dogmas are based on events. Read over your creed: "I believe in Jesus Christ...who was crucified under Pontius Pilate,...and who rose from the dead on the third day." Here the beginnings of the faith are also its foundations.'[1]

The Benedictine scholar Mabillon (whose publication in 1681 of *De Re Diplomatica* is saluted by Bloch as a great year 'in the history of the human mind, for the criticism of the documents of archives was definitely established'[2]), issued a decade later his *Traité des Études Monastiques*, which included a chapter 'De l'étude de l'histoire sacrée et profane',[3] in which the author laid down thirteen principles of historical criticism, only two of which could have perturbed Professor Merrill. The first duty of the historian was to ascertain 'the qualities of a writer; whether he is skilful and sincere, for what ends and with what motive he has written, and whether he is not attached to some party', as (for example) in Mabillon's judgement—and also that of Baronius—Eusebius was to the Arians, Socrates and Sozomen to the Novatians, and Theodoret to Theodore of Mopsuestia. Next, the historian must determine whether the writer whom he studies was contemporary with the events with which he dealt, whether he was an original or secondary authority, and whether he was judicious or too much given to conjecture. 'For, all other things being equal, the opinion of a contemporary writer must be preferred to a more recent. I say, all other things being equal; for it may happen and does sometimes happen, that a writer who is not contemporary, has used good and reliable memoirs, that he is diligent, grave and judicious, and that on the other hand a contemporary writer may be careless, ill-informed or have allowed himself to be corrupted by flattery or by interest.' For this reason the silence of contemporary or near-contemporary writers must not be pressed too far; since a writer of later date may have consulted reliable memoirs which were kept secret at the time of the events which they related, or may have read authors whose works have been lost. But when neither contemporaries nor writers within one or two centuries mention a fact, which a later writer affirms without any authority, credit should not be attached to this later writer, since to do so would open the door to all kinds of error and falsity. Similarly, care should be taken to discern forgeries and pseudo-authorities on the one hand, whilst on the other hand not rejecting a writer for minor faults of misunderstanding, or passion, or barbarity of style, or other natural defects, provided that he is otherwise diligent and upright. Furthermore copyists, abbreviators and annalists should not be despised. In weighing the credit of divergent accounts, the merit rather than the number of the authorities should be considered: 'for it may happen oft-times that the authority of a single writer, who is grave, skilful and sincere, should be preferred to the testimony of a hundred others of little credit, who have copied one from another without discussion or discernment. But this wise choice of authorities depends on a ripe judgement and on the sound instinct of readers, perfected by habit and experience and by reference to a wise and moderate critic.' For this reason, Mabillon cautioned, little attention should be paid to legends of the saints. 'For though I make the observation with pain, I admit with sorrow that profane writers have been more accurate in writing the lives of pagans than many Christians those of our saints.' Nevertheless the other extreme of too great scepticism should also be avoided. 'Ce sont deux extrémités qu'il faut également éviter: et de ne rien croire que très difficilement et de croire trop facilement.' Attention should be paid to three rules proposed by Melchior Cano for distinguishing good historians from inferior: first, a certain integrity which makes them incapable of deceiving their public; secondly, the quality of judgement and discernment which not only delivers them from the will to lie, but gives a ripeness of discrimination and a careful exactitude in examining affairs in order not to accept everything recorded; and thirdly, the giving credit to writers approved by the Church and rejecting those not possessed of this cachet; though Mabillon hastened to add the caveat that some authors on the Index have incurred censure for trivial faults which did not detract from the value of the rest of their work.

Apart from this last article, little criticism could be offered of these rules for the Church historian's exercise of his calling. Perhaps, therefore, the suspicions entertained of his veracity and judgement rest upon a deeper scepticism, the suggestion that his subject-matter itself is partial and apologetic in character. Furthermore, must not the ecclesiastical historian be himself persuaded of the truth of the religion whose history he would set forth, and be consequently biased in his presentation? These questions reach down indeed to the foundations of his craft. Is it necessary that the Church historian must hold the orthodox doctrine of the Person of Christ as a condition of discharging his responsibility? Newman allowed the contrary in his lament that 'the chief, perhaps the only English writer who has any claim to be considered an ecclesiastical historian is the infidel Gibbon'.[1] It is self-evident, moreover, that many specialised studies of particular episodes in Church history may be undertaken without involvement in theological issues. Thus the mundane story of how

> Rome's mitred prelates ambled o'er the Alps
> to hold the Gallic provinces, whose overlords
> their missioners had won to the confession of Christ,

might be described adequately by an unbeliever's pen; nor would the biographer of Wolsey, or Richelieu, or Talleyrand be constrained to concern himself overmuch with theology or even with the principles of Christian ethics. But in the wider context of the whole history of the Church militant here in earth, and in the face of Goethe's solemn affirmation of *das eigentliche, einzige und tiefste Thema der Welt- und Menschengeschichte, dem alle übrigen untergeordnet sind, der Konflikt des Unglaubens und des Glaubens*, it is almost impossibly difficult for the ecclesiastical historian to assume an attitude of indifferent neutrality. A history of music written by Dr Johnson, who confessed that 'it excites in my mind no ideas and hinders me from contemplating my own', would be a strange composition; qualifying perhaps for the verdict which he himself passed upon a performer's rendering of a very difficult piece, 'I would it had been impossible'.[1] It is conceivable to write the history of the Church as that of a great delusion; but it is overwhelmingly probable that the ecclesiastical historian will, and should, be possessed of 'a conviction (such as we often take for granted in other departments of learning) of the *reality* of the thing, the history whereof we are tracing'.[2] In the words of Baronius *sic res gestas recensebimus, ut ecclesiastica ecclesiastice pertractemus*. But this persuasion of the truth of Christianity, whose organised expression in the visible church it is the ecclesiastical historian's province to portray, must impose on him an even stricter standard of accuracy and care in the criticism of his sources, the weighing of their evidence and the evaluation of their reliability. Baronius aspired not merely to equal but to surpass Thucydides in the accuracy of his statements; and also, whilst avoiding the misunderstanding shown by pagan writers concerning Church history, to escape the credulity of some ecclesiastical writers.[1]

But if the Church historian equals his secular colleague in integrity and accuracy, what of the sources upon which his study is founded? Are they inadequate when weighed by modern processes of historical criticism? It must be granted unequivocally that, beginning with the New Testament, these sources are written by believers for believers, being set down to give readers 'the certainty concerning the things' wherein they had been orally instructed. The earliest, the Acts of the Apostles, depicts the apostolic Church as setting forth its *raison d'être* in the declaration that 'Jesus of Nazareth, a man approved of God among you,...ye have taken and have crucified and slain, whom God hath raised up,...and hath made that same Jesus...both Lord and Christ'.[2] Here at once the ecclesiastical historian is confronted by two issues, whose satisfactory solution is vital to the discharge of his responsibility. First, the declaration combines inextricably fact with interpretation, and, secondly, it raises the question whether the particular interpretation was that of the primitive Church or of Jesus himself. At the present time it would doubtless be an otiose exercise in slaying the slain, to amass arguments in refutation of the thesis that 'history is a science, no less and no more'; though it would be pertinent to recall the aspiration behind the maxim, namely that history might establish its kinship with 'the sciences which deal objectively with the facts of the universe'.[1] It is now generally admitted, as R. G. Collingwood argued, that

> the historian, investigating any event in the past, makes a distinction between what may be called the outside and the inside of an event. By the outside of the event, I mean everything belonging to it which can be described in terms of bodies and their movements: the passage of Caesar accompanied by certain men across the Rubicon on one day, or the spilling of his blood on the floor of the Senate House at another. By the inside of the event I mean that in it which can only be described in terms of thought: Caesar's defiance of Republican law, or the clash of constitutional policy between himself and his assassins. The historian is never concerned with either of these to the exclusion of the other. He is investigating not mere events (where by an event I mean one which has only an outside and no inside), but actions; and an action is the unity of the outside with the inside of an event. He is interested in the crossing of the Rubicon only in its relation to Republican law, and in the spilling of Caesar's blood only in relation to a constitutional conflict. His work may begin by discovering the outside of an event, but it can never end there; he must always remember that the event was an action, and that his main task is to think himself into this action, to discern the thought of its agent.[2]

The principle of this argument was accepted by Marc Bloch, who, commenting on the dictum of Bayle that 'no valid objection will ever be raised to the fact that Caesar defeated Pompey', remarked that 'if there were no certainty except for a few facts of this type, devoid of explanation, history would be reduced to a series of rough notations, without much intellectual value. Happily this is not the case'; and he concluded that 'in the last analysis it is human consciousness which is the subject-matter of history'.[1] A parallel affirmation in respect of Christian history to that of Bayle concerning Caesar and Pompey, may be found in the laconic sentence of Tacitus, *Auctor nominis eius Christus Tiberio imperitante per procuratorem Pontium Pilatum supplicio adfectus erat.* Such a statement provides no clue to the meaning of the event, but rather goes far to establish the truth that interpretation is no refractory element, improperly introduced by the historian into his narrative of facts, but an indispensable part of his responsibility.

If therefore the appeal is prosecuted from Tacitus to the New Testament, it becomes immediately evident that the death of Jesus was the culmination of an acute conflict between himself and the Jewish religious hierarchy, centring in his claim to be the Messiah and their rejection of it and their consequent contrivance of his crucifixion. Accordingly, the narratives of the Gospels, and particularly the Passion-narratives, present the ministry and teaching of Jesus within the framework of messiahship and as the detailed fulfilment of Old Testament prophecy. There is nothing unhistorical (not to say anti-historical) in this interpenetration of fact with interpretation; but the question arises whether the claim to messiahship was made by Jesus himself or only by the primitive Church. If the latter, the historical foundations of Christianity are severely shaken, since a far-reaching historical scepticism shrouds the life and teaching of its Founder. The question is raised at the present time from the side of theologians, since under the impetus of the school of Form-critics the former 'quest of the historical Jesus' has given place to investigation of the part played by the apologetic, didactic and pastoral needs of the primitive Church in fashioning both form and content of the Gospels.

It is not without interest, therefore, to observe that Form-criticism as a method of literary analysis has dominated New Testament study at a time when in other fields it has been discarded as unsatisfactory. 'In field after field' of literary studies, as Dr Helen Gardner remarks in her fascinating Riddell Lectures, 'theories of composite authorship, earlier versions and different strata have been discarded....The assumption today is more and more in favour of single authorship, unless there is clear external evidence to the contrary....The importance of the single author and the single work dominates literary studies....“Schools and influences” are out of fashion.' Indeed, she observes that 'it is interesting that so many scholars working independently and in widely different fields, have felt the hypothesis of single authorship to be the obvious and fruitful one....Trends in literary scholarship thus give support to critics who regard it as their duty to see works as integrated wholes, and the body of an author's work as a totality proceeding from a single mind.'[1] Since, therefore, the critical study of the Gospels is not an exercise *in vacuo*, unrelated to other spheres of literary criticism, Dr Gardner proceeds justifiably to apply her conclusions to this field. 'Form-criticism, particularly in its extremer manifestations, is not congenial to the temper of mind which regards it as the first duty of the critic to make sense of literary wholes. It disintegrates the separate Gospels and is open to the literary objection that it is not dealing with the work itself, but with the materials out of which it was made; and these materials, the oral preaching of the Apostles, do not exist; they are irrecoverable except by deductions from what we have. It can be complained that the Form-critic has reduced St Mark to a mere piecer-and-stitcher-together of materials already given him by others.'[2] Furthermore, this method of criticism 'does nothing to illuminate, and indeed evaporates, St Mark's sense of what we mean by historical reality, the "Here and Now" of our daily experience, the "Then and There" of memory, by which I do not mean detailed precision of testimony, but the deep sense of "happening". Indeed the method is often oblivious of, and impatient with, the historical. Whoever wrote the Gospel of St Mark was a man, not a disembodied imagination.... What differentiates his Gospel from all other messages of salvation, is the assertion that something has happened in the world of history.' Finally, Dr Gardner concludes that 'as literary criticism I cannot regard the new symbolical or typological approach to the Gospels as satisfactory. It does not explain a prime historical fact: that for centuries Christian emotion directed towards the historic person of Jesus, true God and true Man, has found in the Gospels the strength of its own conviction that "Christ walked on this earth".'[1]

Dr Gardner further draws attention to the contrast made by Professor Auerbach between the *Odyssey* and the historical narratives of the Old Testament on the one hand, as showing that 'the difference between legend and history is in most cases easily perceived by a reasonably experienced reader'; and between Petronius and Tacitus on the other hand and St Mark's record of the denial of Christ by St Peter, as illustrating the difference between rhetoric and concrete historical actuality.[2] If, however, it is deemed temerarious for students of history and literature to trespass upon the ground of Gospel-criticism, it may be noticed that Professor T. W. Manson, in one of his last essays, expressed the conviction that Form-criticism 'has by now done about all that it could do, and more than it ought'; and therefore that 'there is a good deal to be said for treating the Gospels as historical documents concerning Jesus of Nazareth rather than psychological case-material concerning the early Christians'; and he concluded that the duty of critics was to return to 'the business of treating the Gospels—as wholes and in detail—as historical documents, using all the resources of exact scholarship and strict historical method for the task'.[3]

The same principle is true also of the earliest Christian essay in historiography, the Acts of the Apostles. Notwithstanding its insoluble issues—the tantalising lack of chronology in its first twelve chapters, the extremely selective character of its record, which leaves unanswered questions whose name is legion and which the modern Church historian would fain put to the author, and the unresolved conflict between its account of St Paul's movements and theology and the evidence dispersed in the Pauline Epistles—the Acts may still claim a historical character and its writer the title of 'the first Christian historian'. Such a recognition embraces the fact that St Luke's purpose is theological also, and that his selection and presentation of his material are governed by certain dominating presuppositions: namely, that the salient features of early Church history were the mission to the Gentiles and the consequent breach between Christianity and Judaism, the parts played by both St Peter and St Paul in this process, the historical and theological bases of primitive Christian apologetic as expounded in the speeches which St Luke puts into the mouths of the two chief Apostles, and the twin foci of this Gentile mission in the visit of St Paul to Athens and his arrival in Rome. Granted the soundness of the author's principles of selection, the Acts may claim a truly historical character, despite its lacunae.

The gratitude of students of Church history to the author of the Acts is increased, moreover, by the darkness which descended upon the landscape after its conclusion and which lasted virtually until the *Ecclesiastical History* of Eusebius. Furthermore, for the period from the sub-apostolic age until his own days, Eusebius was dependent upon the gatherings of a gleaner, so that he has been called 'rather a compiler of extracts than a writer of history';[1] and valuable though his extracts are, their fragmentary and partial character may be seen, for example, from the paucity of references to Cyprian of Carthage and the little detailed knowledge of the development of the Church of Rome—two issues which were to become of crucial interest and importance in the controversies of the Reformation and post-Reformation centuries. In other respects also, and in regard to events with which he was contemporary, Eusebius has been the subject of criticism. Baronius held that 'having been once very much imbued with Arianism, Eusebius, although he may be held reliable in other matters, in those relating to the doctrines of the Arians, as likewise in events concerning the emperor Constantine, has set down many things falsely'. The same censure was directed at his successors. 'Socrates equally, being addicted to the sect of the Novatians, was defective in veracity, and Sozomen was tarred with the same brush.' Even less favourable was Baronius' opinion of later ecclesiastical historians. 'For if you should consult later historians of ecclesiastical affairs, you will certainly perceive a large class amongst them, who without discrimination have set down whatever came to hand from the writings of others or they themselves had received by report, and without any further investigation of the truth, have often mingled together absurd fables, old-wives' tales and vulgar rumours, to the great prejudice of other matters resting upon a solid foundation.'[1] From such extremes of credulity, if not from a parallel partiality for some particular theological and ecclesiastical standpoint, the Church historians of the sixteenth and seventeenth centuries aspired to be emancipated.

There remains another difficult problem to vex the Church historian. From the Acts of the Apostles onwards (and indeed backwards also in the Gospels) his literary sources contain a liberal element of the miraculous. 'Besides the occasional prodigies', observed Gibbon ironically, 'which might sometimes be effected by the immediate interposition of the Deity, when he suspended the laws of Nature for the service of religion, the Christian Church from the time of the Apostles and their first disciples, has claimed an uninterrupted succession of miraculous powers.' The sceptical satirist knew whereof he wrote; for his own youthful and transient conversion to Rome had been due in part to his 'implicit belief that the gift of miraculous powers was continued in the Church during the first four or five centuries of Christianity', and to the conclusion deduced therefrom 'that miracles are the test of truth and that the Church must be orthodox and pure which was so often approved by the visible interposition of the Deity'.[2] Eusebius indeed related the story of the Thundering Legion; but apart from this instance, was by no means credulous of miraculous events and referred to them comparatively rarely. After quoting the testimony of Irenaeus to the miracles which 'had remained in some churches even as far as his time', his conclusion might be interpreted as evidence that he thought them to have ceased in his own day.[1] His successors, Socrates and Sozomen, were much more credulous in this matter; and although towards the end of the fourth century St Hilary of Poitiers in the west observed that in his own time miracles had ceased, and the authentic *Acta Martyrum* are remarkably free from them, these were exceptions to the general tendency both in paganism and Christianity to multiply supernatural phenomena. Indeed, not until the rise of the scientific movement in the latter half of the seventeenth century did a decisive change come over the intellectual climate of educated countries in this respect.

In more modern times the progress of historical criticism has considerably reduced the scope of the problem. 'Presque tous les documents', remarked Langlois and Seignobos at the end of the last century, 'qui rapportent des faits miraculeux sont déjà suspects par ailleurs'; but even where this was not the case, they held all such things wholly incredible. 'Les observations contenues dans les documents historiques ne valent jamais celles des savants contemporains....La méthode historique indirecte ne vaut jamais les méthodes des sciences d'observation. Si ses résultats sont en désaccord avec les leurs, c'est elle qui doit céder.'[1] Perhaps this attitude may constitute an example of the survival—noted by F. R. Tennant—of 'the suspicion, cast out of science, that Nature is so rigidly uniform that any breach of uniformity asserted in the gospel-record is necessarily fictitious'.[2] Notwithstanding the results of historical criticism, however, the Church historian is left with a sufficient element of the supernatural to challenge interpretation, and must admit that *qua* historian he can pronounce no verdict. 'Whether the appearance of the cross of light', observes Professor Norman Baynes in respect of the conversion of Constantine, 'was only a subjective appearance, or whether it was objective reality, the historian cannot decide. Still less can he determine whether it was a God-granted miracle. To answer such a question, the historian must turn philosopher or theologian: as historian he is perforce silent. He is unable to affirm miracle; but most certainly he cannot deny it. Just as in the case with Paul on the road to Damascus, so with Constantine in his hour of crisis, the historian can but discuss the value of his sources and state the result of his criticism.'[3]

The mention of St Paul raises a further consideration of fundamental importance for the Church historian. The author of the Acts, as Foakes-Jackson remarked, notwithstanding his purpose 'to describe the foundation and development of an institution', was 'perforce compelled to dwell on the influence of individuals in the development of the Church; and here in a nutshell is the real problem of the writing of church history'.[1] The author of the *Magdeburg Centuries* indeed made this a ground of criticism of the early historians of the Church: *tantum sunt personales, ut sic dicamus, historici.* But the record of ecclesiastical history is studded with such religious events as the conversions of Paul, Augustine, Francis of Assisi, Luther, Loyola and Wesley (to name but a few out of many), whose influence upon history is writ in such large letters that he who runs may read, and whose results are cogent evidence of the importance of the individual. If Sir Maurice Powicke is correct in affirming that history 'is in its nature an emphatic denial of fatalism', and if Sir Isaiah Berlin in his philippic against all theories of 'historical inevitability' is justified in his conclusion that 'for historians, determinism is not a serious issue', much of the credit may not unjustly be claimed for ecclesiastical history, since its testimony affords, as Figgis insisted, 'the supreme refutation of the impersonal view of history'.[2] Even Bury recognised that his desire to conform history to the pattern of the physical sciences was challenged by 'the heel of Achilles in all historical speculations of this class', namely, 'the role of the individual'; and gave as a particular example the policy of the emperor Constantine towards the Church. 'The audacity of Constantine the Great in exalting Christianity to the dominant place cannot be sufficiently emphasised.' Substantially the same conclusion is voiced by Professor Norman Baynes: 'Constantine can only be satisfactorily interpreted in terms of the *Zeitgeist*, if the *Zeitgeist* is arbitrarily fashioned in the likeness of Constantine. The more closely Constantine's life and achievements are studied, the more inevitably is one driven to see in them an erratic block which has diverted the stream of human history.'[1] Furthermore, the Church historian may claim to see in such episodes evidence that, as a matter of sober historical fact,

> There's a Divinity doth shape our ends
> Rough-hew them how we will.

For, save at the price of making nonsense of his records and thereby conceding the materialist interpretation of the process of history, the ecclesiastical historian may not surrender his conviction of the reality of the influence upon men of the Spirit of God, who thus by divers portions and in divers manners has spoken unto our fathers after the flesh.

In addition to his testimony to the influence of individuals in the fashioning of history, the Church historian must likewise emphasise the uniqueness of events. History indeed is concerned by its nature with 'particular, concrete or once-occurring events', and 'revealed religion is mediated by unique events, occurring at particular dates and places'.[2] Thus on the one hand Sir Maurice Powicke defines history as concerned with 'events which have their own right, so to speak, to exist, because they are informed, as a body is informed by a soul, by human intelligence'; and on the other hand Dr Clement Webb held that religion 'is concerned pre-eminently with concrete, historical, individual facts and relations'.[3]

The subject of ecclesiastical history indeed is a society which from its foundation has affirmed its unique character as an elect race, a royal priesthood, and a holy people; and which was soon recognised by its opponents as a 'third race', distinct from both Romans and Jews, as Tertullian testified.[1] Moreover, as the bearer of a New Covenant and both heir and fulfilment of the Old Covenant, it interpreted its history in theological terms and categories, as a series of events of unique importance. Sir Isaiah Berlin has observed that 'we select certain events or persons because we believe them to have had a special degree of "influence" or "power" or "importance"';[2] and precisely this claim is made by the Church historian for the events upon which the Christian Church was founded. As Professor Dodd has remarked, 'the particular, even the unique, is a category entirely appropriate to the understanding of history; and since one particular event exceeds another in significance, there may well be an event which is uniquely significant, and this event may give an unique character to the whole series to which it belongs. This is in fact the assertion which Christianity makes. It takes the series of events recorded or reflected in the Bible, from the call of Abraham to the emergence of the Church, and declares that in this series the ultimate reality of all history, which is the purpose of God, is finally revealed, because the series is itself controlled by the supreme event of all—the life, death and resurrection of Jesus Christ.'[3] Similarly, a recent

Gifford lecturer has averred, from the standpoint of theology, that the Christian revelation 'should not be thought of as a system of divinely-communicated truths to be accepted on authority as complement to what we can learn by our own study of what actually exists and happens. It comes by taking certain events in the history of the world as of unique and supreme significance for our understanding of all things.'[1] Historically the Church has conceived its function as guarding and transmitting those *gesta Dei per Christum* wrought *propter nos homines et propter nostram salutem*; and this deposit is contained both in the written canonical books of Scripture and in the oral tradition of the Church itself.

Whereas therefore, on the one hand, the historical character of the Christian revelation gives to the Church historian a status of unique importance and influence, on the other hand *qua* historian he cannot pronounce on the correctness of the theological interpretation of the events in question. 'He may conceivably be able...to prove that a given interpretation of the facts as they simply happened, is the most primitive that we can trace. But when all this has been done, it remains a further question whether the primitive interpretation is the true, or the most probable, interpretation....Thus the problem involves a question which lies outside the sphere of historical investigation and criticism.'[2] As was noted by a patristic commentator on John i. 6 ('There was a man sent from God whose name was John'), the historical career of John the Baptist is a question of fact, to be ascertained by the usual processes of historical investigation, and to which the unbeliever in his divine mission may subscribe no less than the believer. But the interpretation that 'he was sent from God' is an act of faith. 'Those who hold it, do so as a consequence of faith; and for those who do not hold it by faith, it remains either a matter of doubt or of contemptuous disbelief.' If this be true of the forerunner *a fortiori* it is even more evident in the case of Him to whom John pointed. 'It would seem to follow', as A. E. Taylor argued in his Gifford Lectures, 'that the utmost we can do by an appeal to the records is no more than to show that it is possible and permissible to interpret the recorded acts and teaching of our Lord in a way which does not conflict with the claims Christian theology makes for his Person. Hostile criticism can be shown not to have made out its case; it seems doubtful whether empirical methods can show more than this. The specifically Christian "faith" in the Person of Christ can be defended against attacks based on unfriendly interpretation of the records of his life and teaching, but not adequately substantiated by examination of those records.'[1]

Nor does the question rest with the close of the Canon of Scripture. During the first five centuries of the history of the Church both doctrine and organisation were the subject of development; and to the general principles and pattern of this development all parties, Romanist and non-Romanist, to the controversies arising from the Reformation movement made their appeal. The ecclesiastical historian, since he must needs concern himself with the theological interpretation of the events which are the subject of his study, may, and should, properly be also a student of historical theology, that is, of dogma; just as the constitutional historian must be familiar with the history of law and the economic historian with the principles of economics. But, though he must turn theologian when discussing the truth of the interpretation placed upon events, where the issues at stake involve properly historical matters, such as the investigation of sources and the assessment of their evidence, he must claim an independent right of voice and vote. Furthermore, when the Vincentian canon, that 'in the Catholic Church we take the greatest care to hold that which has been believed everywhere, always and by all', secured general acceptance, the Church historian became in some wise a court of appeal. For it lay within his proper province to determine whether there was an adequate and sufficient amount of historical evidence for an alleged event which was itself the basis of a dogma, and whether a particular doctrine had in fact been held *ubique, semper et ab omnibus*. With equal modesty and conviction the ecclesiastical historian must apply to his study of the Church the aphorism of Cicero: *historia cum magistra vitae est, tum lux veritatis*.

CHAPTER II

THE PETRINE PRIMACY:

IRENAEUS AND CYPRIAN AT THE COUNCILS OF TRENT AND THE VATICAN

'In Scriptures there is no mention made of Peter's supremacy, and Eusebius in *Ecclesiastica Historia* reporteth that Clement in Sexto libro Dispositionum affirmed that Peter, John and James after the Ascension of our Saviour, although he had set them almost above all the apostles, yet they took not the glory of supremacy upon them, but that James which is called Justus was ordained the bishop of the apostles.'[1] When so conservative a bishop as Stephen Gardiner could write thus of the Petrine primacy in *De Vera Obedientia Oratio*, it needed little gift of prophecy to perceive that during the century following its publication the question of papal prerogatives would occupy the forefront of the controversial stage, and would exercise exhaustively the pens of both Protestant and Romanist divines. This was indeed a natural characteristic and consequence of the sixteenth-century Reformation. For despite many differences of faith and polity between the churches affected by that revolution, all had agreed in rejecting the claims of the papacy, in both their theoretical and practical expressions. On this issue, more perhaps than on any other, the testimony of history was of crucial significance; and it was moreover a matter which involved the fundamental question of the relationship of history and theology, since the primacy of the see of Rome rested upon the evidence of early Church history on the one hand and on the exegesis of certain New Testament texts on the other. Attacks on the outworks of the papal position had begun a century earlier, notably by the demonstration in 1440 by the Italian humanist, Lorenzo Valla, of the forgery of the Donation of Constantine, which had been so useful a weapon in the papal armoury against the empire and had been accepted as genuine by Occam and Marsilio of Padua. When Johannes Cochlaeus discovered this treatise at Bologna and communicated it to Ulrich von Hutten, the latter published it in 1518 with a satirical dedication to Leo X, after which it was frequently reissued during the next two decades.

The assault on papal pretensions, however, penetrated much more deeply than Valla's *De falso credita et ementita Donatione Constantini declamatio*, and shortly the whole complex of questions concerning the residence and episcopate of St Peter at Rome was raised. At the outset, Luther in the Leipzig disputation maintained a comparatively moderate position in respect of the Roman primacy. In his *Resolutio super propositione XIII de potestate Papae* of 1519 he accepted the fact of the papal primacy, whilst throwing into question its causes and origins and the adequacy of the proofs by which it was supported. Further he contended that it was of human, not divine, authority; and that it embraced two distinct things, a primacy of honour and one of power; of which, whilst accepting the former as descending to the popes as successors of St Peter, he denied that the latter had been given to the prince of the Apostles.[1] Calvin, however, in the *Institutes of the Christian Religion* presented a more thoroughgoing conspectus of the question. Beginning by a denial that the primacy of Rome took its origin either in the institution of Christ or in the practice of the early Church, he differentiated between the position of St Peter as 'first among the faithful', and the deduction therefrom that he enjoyed a primacy over others, accepting the former whilst rejecting the latter. Moreover, even if the latter were conceded, it did not follow that from a single example, a universal rule or a perpetual enactment could be concluded. Furthermore, the first see of St Peter was at Antioch, and the statement of Eusebius that Peter presided over the Church at Rome for twenty-five years could easily be refuted; wherefore Calvin accordingly concluded that 'from this agreement of authors, I do not dispute that he died there, but that he was a bishop, particularly for a long period, I cannot believe'.[2] Instead he offered three reasons for the high honour ascribed to Rome in the ante-Nicene period, namely, the tradition of its Petrine foundation, its position as the seat of empire, and its stability during the doctrinal disputes culminating in the Council of Nicaea.

The ground was thus prepared for a rejection of the contemporary claims of the papacy; and not only the assertion of a *plenitudo potestatis* in Boniface VIII's *Unam Sanctam*, but also the question of the origins of the Roman primacy and the historical evidence for the episcopate of St Peter at Rome became the subject of controversial examination. The biblical evidence concerning St Peter's connexion with Rome was admittedly exiguous. An uncertain passage in the Apocalypse (Rev. xi. 3–13), especially the references to 'my two witnesses' and to the circumstance that 'their dead bodies lie in the street of the great city, which spiritually is called Sodom and Egypt, where also their Lord was crucified'; and a solitary mention in I Peter v. 13 that 'she that is in Babylon saluteth you', interpreted of the Church in Rome, constituted all the scriptural testimony. Appeal was accordingly made to the early history and tradition of the Church, particularly to Clement of Rome, Ignatius, Irenaeus and Cyprian. Unfortunately the situation was much confused by the widespread acceptance in the sixteenth century of the apocryphal works ascribed to Clement and to Dionysius the Areopagite. Roman Catholic writers generally regarded the *Apostolic Constitutions* and *Canons* and the *Recognitions* as authentic writings of Clement, whilst not only Eck in his controversy with Luther, but also the Council of Trent and the Sorbonne defended the works attributed to Dionysius, who was regarded as an actual disciple of St Paul. It remained for the seventeenth century to throw light on these dark places by differentiating between authentic and pseudonymous works. In 1633 Patrick Young published at Oxford the First Epistle of Clement; and in 1644 Ussher published his edition of the Epistles of Ignatius, which was followed by that of Isaac Voss in 1646, which provoked a considerable controversy, in the course of which three Huguenot scholars, Saumaise, Blondel and Daillé assailed the authenticity of the seven Ignatian Epistles, until the dispute was virtually determined by the appearance in 1672 of Pearson's *Vindiciae Epistolarum S. Ignatii*. With the critical weapons thus forged the debate could proceed on firmer foundations; and the testimony of Clement, Ignatius, Irenaeus and Cyprian concerning the Roman primacy became the subject of polemical study. Therewith also Church history entered into its heritage as an indispensable court of appeal in the controversy between Romanist and Protestant.

In regard to I Clement, its evidence likewise was equivocal and uncertain. In the fifth section there occurred an oblique mention of the martyrdoms of St Peter and St Paul: 'Let us take the noble examples of our own generation. Through jealousy and envy the greatest and most righteous pillars of the Church were persecuted and contended unto death. Let us set before our eyes the good apostles: Peter, who because of unrighteous jealousy suffered not one or two but many trials, and having thus given his testimony, went to the glorious place which was his due. Through jealousy and strife Paul showed the way to the prize of endurance.'[1] Apart, however, from the prestige thus accruing to the Roman Church from this fact of its having been the scene of the deaths of the two apostles associated with its early history, this testimony contributed nothing to the papal claims. Nor did the equally vague mention in the Epistle of Ignatius to the Romans carry the matter further: 'I do not order you as did Peter and Paul; they were Apostles, I am a convict; they were free, I am even until now a slave.'[2] Indeed Lightfoot commented that 'in Clement's letter itself—the earliest document issuing from the Roman Church after apostolic times—no mention is made of episcopacy properly so called....It does not proceed from the bishop of Rome, but from the Church of Rome'; whilst in respect of Ignatius' letter, 'we might read the epistle from beginning to end without a suspicion that the episcopal office existed in Rome at this time, if we had no other grounds for the belief'. If therefore I Clement could be described by Batiffol as 'l'épiphanie de la primauté Romaine', and by Lightfoot as 'the first step towards papal domination', it was in the sense that 'it was originally a primacy not of the episcopate, but of the church'.[3]

In this connexion the testimony of Irenaeus invited especial scrutiny, and the conflict of interpretation of the passage in *Adv. Haereses* III, 3, 2 was joined between Protestant and Romanist, particularly after the publication in 1526 of Erasmus' edition of the works of Irenaeus. In the controverted passage, Irenaeus appealed to the succession in 'the very great and very ancient and universally-known church founded and established at Rome by the two apostles Peter and Paul', against the Gnostic claim to a secret tradition; and continued: *Ad hanc enim ecclesiam propter potentiorem principalitatem necesse est omnem convenire ecclesiam, hoc est, eos qui sunt fideles, in qua semper ab his qui sunt undique, conservata est ea quae est ab apostolis traditio.* Two variant expositions of *potentiorem principalitatem*, of *convenire ad*, and of *qui sunt undique* were offered, giving differing interpretations of the meaning of the passage. The one understood *potentiorem principalitatem* as referring to the imperial pre-eminence of the city of Rome, translated *convenire ad* as 'resort to', and construed the final sentence, 'inasmuch as the apostolic tradition is always preserved by the faithful who are everywhere'. Thus a picture was presented of the Church of Rome as a microcosm of Christendom, to which the faithful of every church must come by reason of the business bringing them to the imperial city, and which therefore represented the whole of Christendom in virtue of those members of other churches residing there and witnessing with the Roman Church to the apostolic tradition. The other interpretation saw in the *potentiorem principalitatem* a reference to the primacy of the Roman Church, translated *convenire ad* as 'agree with', and understood the concluding phrase as indicating that in the Church of Rome 'the tradition which comes from the Apostles is always preserved by the faithful who are everywhere', portraying thereby the test of adherence to the apostolic tradition on the part of other churches as their agreement with the Church of Rome.

Thus on the one side the French scholars, Jean Driedo in *De Scripturis et dogmatibus ecclesiasticis* and Jacques Latomus in *De Primatu Pontificis*,[1] and also Albert Pighius, Provost of St John's Church, Utrecht, in *Hierarchiae Ecclesiasticae Assertio*, interpreted the passage in favour of the Roman primacy. Driedo and Latomus emphasised the obligation of all churches not only to maintain union with Rome, but also to recognise this *Ecclesia apostolica* as the source of their own episcopacy; and Pighius affirmed the necessity for the universal church to conform in matters of faith with the Roman Church.[2] Similarly the Franciscan François Feuardent, in his edition of the works of Irenaeus, described the Church of Rome as 'the head and rule of all the churches', to which by divine appointment the churches of Europe, Africa, Alexandria, Asia and the east were subject, in respect both of its jurisdiction and authority and also of its orthodox faith.[3] On the other side Flacius Illyricus in the principal work of Protestant polemic, the *Magdeburg Centuries*, after denying that Ignatius knew anything of the obligation of other churches to be subject to Rome, interpreted the words of Irenaeus as referring solely to agreement in the doctrine handed down from the Apostles without any further implication.[4] Nor have modern studies resulted in unanimity amongst scholars. The substitution in the Clermont manuscript of *potiorem* for *potentiorem principalitatem*, with the suggested translation 'superior origin' does not solve the problem; nor has it met with universal approval. On the one hand it has been argued that Irenaeus was borrowing a convention of historians of the Hellenistic age, with whom 'the argument from the position of the city of Rome is a commonplace', and that he was therefore 'simply reproducing a well-worn rhetorical commonplace'.[1] On the other hand *propter potentiorem principalitatem* has been interpreted as implying 'un degré plus éminent d'apostolicité'; *qui sunt undique* as a deliberate repetition 'pour accenter l'idée d'universalité, d'unanimité dans la croyance, idée contenue dans *omnem ecclesiam*, et déjà soulignée une première fois par cette addition: *hoc est eos qui sunt undique*'; and *in qua ab his* has been the subject of 'une interprétation très plausible, qui, une fois admise, fortifie singulièrement la thèse de la prééminence romaine: c'est celle qui fait la préposition *in* synonyme de *per*; et par conséquent l'expression d'une causalité instrumentale ou ministérielle'.[2] More recently the revolutionary interpretation that Irenaeus was writing of the universal Church and without reference to the Church of Rome, has been advanced by Pierre Nautin. On the grounds of style, conformity with contemporary Church history, and agreement with the context of Irenaeus' work, Nautin concluded that critics had disputed for four centuries 'sur une phrase qui n'en valait pas la peine', since the controverted passage was 'une vérité banale, simple affirmation du principe qui est à la base de la doctrine conciliaire; il est nécessaire que toute église soit unie a l'Église universelle'.[1]

In view of the verdict of not proven in respect of the testimony of Irenaeus, it was to be expected that the principal court of appeal should be the writings of Cyprian of Carthage. At the Leipzig Disputation in 1519 Luther cited several of St Cyprian's Epistles as evidence that he recognised no primacy of jurisdiction in the see of Rome: 'If the reverend doctor [Eck] wishes to stand on the authority of Cyprian, we shall conclude the disputation at this hour. For Cyprian never addresses Cornelius otherwise than as most dear brother'; and again, 'Cyprian always addresses Cornelius as brother, and never as Lord.[2]' Luther interpreted the theory that the unity of the episcopate proceeded from Rome as relating only to the western Church; and he quoted Cyprian's letters as establishing the unity of the Church on the basis not of the Roman primacy but on that of one Lord, one faith, one baptism, since Cyprian held it a tyranny for other bishops to be compelled by one bishop to obedience.[3] When Eck drew his attention to the passage in Cyprian's *De Ecclesiae Unitate C. IV*, declaring that 'the rest of the apostles were exactly what Peter was, endowed with an equal share of office and power, but there was unity at the beginning before any development, to demonstrate that the Church of Christ is one', Luther replied by arguing that the Apostles rightly gave to Peter an honorary precedence, but that each of them in his own status, and therefore every bishop in his own diocese, was of equal honour.[1] Calvin likewise cited this passage as proof that Christ did not place one man above all the rest, but set forth the unity of the Church; adding that Cyprian described this unity in most appropriate words, 'the episcopate is a single whole, in which each bishop's share gives him a right to, and a responsibility for, the whole'. Calvin also quoted Cyprian frequently as giving to Cornelius the titles of 'brother', 'fellow-bishop' and 'colleague'.[2] Similarly the *Magdeburg Centuries* made great play with Cyprian as an opponent of the papal claims. Flacius Illyricus illustrated Cyprian's view of the Roman primacy from his calling Cornelius 'brother' and 'bishop'; and from his rebuke to the Roman bishop for receiving letters from Cyprian's opponents instead of referring them to their own bishop, in which connexion Cyprian firmly asserted the authority of the African episcopate; whilst Flacius further denied that Cyprian's reference in Letter LIX to 'the chair of Peter and the principal church from which the unity of the episcopate derives' implied recognition of Rome's primacy and headship over other churches *jure divino*. On the contrary Cyprian interpreted the unity of the Church as consisting in the concurrence of all the churches and bishops in doctrine and discipline.[3]

Thus far indeed the Protestants seemed to have found in Cyprian an invaluable support for their position in repudiating papal jurisdiction. For, notwithstanding his citation in *De Ecclesiae Unitate* of the Petrine passages from St Matthew and St John, which were the proof-texts of the papal claims, he had qualified these by his exposition of the episcopate as 'a single whole in which each bishop's share gives him a right to, and a responsibility for, the whole'. In 1563, however, Manutius published for the first time the Primacy Text of Cyprian's work, which differed from the Textus Receptus by certain changes and additions, affirming directly the papal primacy. For, after citing the Petrine text from Matthew xvi. 18–19 and the Dominical command to Peter *Pasce oves meos* from John xxi. 15–17, it continued, 'upon him Christ builds his Church and to him he entrusts the sheep to be fed'. There followed the sentence from the Textus Receptus, 'And although he gives equal power to all the Apostles'; to which was added, 'yet he established one chair, and arranged by his own authority the origin and principle of unity'. After the next sentence—'Certainly the rest of the apostles were exactly what Peter was'—there was inserted: 'but primacy is given to Peter, and one Church and one chair is demonstrated. And they are all shepherds: but the flock is shown to be one, which is to be fed by all the apostles in unanimous agreement. He who deserts the chair of Peter on whom the Church was founded, does he trust that he is in the Church?' The discovery of this Primacy Text was a severe blow to the Protestants and a powerful addition to the papal armoury. In the year following Manutius' work, indeed, there appeared the first publication by Morel of the famous Letter of Firmilian of Caesarea to Cyprian (Letter LXXV), in which the writer launched so terrific a philippic against Pope Stephen; and this did something to redress the balance in favour of the Protestants.

Controversy began shortly therefore concerning the authenticity of the Primacy Text. One of the ablest scholars of the day, Latino Latini, had refused to allow his name to appear in Manutius' edition because of these additions to the Textus Receptus; for whilst admitting their occurrence in some manuscripts, he ascribed them to marginal notes which had later been incorporated into the text. In 1568 Pamelius' edition of Cyprian's works used the Primacy Text, supported by the further evidence of a codex at Cambron in Hainault. The reaction of Protestants to these discoveries may be illustrated from the edition of Cyprian published at Geneva in 1593 by Simon Goulart, who rejected Pamelius' interpretation of Cyprian on the grounds that the latter wrote of the unity of the Church, not of the papal primacy, whereas Pamelius had misinterpreted him by applying his words to the Roman see; and that between the standpoints of the African bishop and Pamelius there was only the relationship of contradiction. The words *Hic Petro primatus datur* Goulart, against Cardinal Hosius, regarded as a marginal gloss, later incorporated in the text. Further he appealed to the Decretum of Gratian as evidence that the additions of the Primacy Text were not authentic, and cited Cyprian's Letters as confirmatory of the view of the Textus Receptus against the Primacy Text.[1]

The controversy was of acute contemporary importance because the concluding sessions of the Council of Trent were much occupied with the question whether the episcopate was of direct institution by Christ or mediately through the papacy, and this involved of course the cognate problem of the relationship of the rest of the Apostles to St Peter. The matter arose from the duty of residence of bishops upon their sees, whether it was by divine or only by ecclesiastical law; and this raised the fundamental issue of the nature of episcopal authority. On 20 April 1562 the question whether residence is of divine obligation was put to the vote; when sixty-seven voted affirmatively, thirty-eight negatively, and thirty-four for reference to the pope. In the following October consideration of decrees and canons concerning the sacrament of Orders brought up the matter again; and during the debates the authority of Cyprian was vigorously claimed on both sides. On 13 October the archbishop of Granada contended that bishops were instituted by divine right by Christ; for if the pope alone had immediate authority from Christ, and if only such authority immediately from Christ was of divine right, then the pope was the only bishop *jure divino*. Against this latter view he cited Cyprian's words *episcopatus unus est*, *cujus a singulis in solidum pars tenetur*.[2] Similarly the bishop of Auria on 19 November affirmed on the authority of Basil, Gregory the Great, Cyprian and other Fathers that the institution of the episcopate by Christ *jure divino* embraced also jurisdiction, that it proceeded from Christ as the fount and principal cause and from him through the pope as through a minister and instrument; and he argued from chapter IV of *De Ecclesiae Unitate* that the promise *Tibi dabo claves regni* was not to Peter alone, but to the other Apostles also.[1] In similar terms the bishop of Orense followed by an appeal to chapters IV and V of Cyprian, *qui episcopatum unum esse dicit*, *id est unam Ecclesiam*; and on the next day the bishop of Lavaux, whilst agreeing that the pope was the successor of Peter, affirmed, as Cyprian had said, that the Apostles had the same authority as Peter.[2] On 25 November the bishop of Almeria, replying to the argument that Cyprian, by admitting the Dominical commission to Peter 'Feed my sheep', had recognised that jurisdiction descended to the bishops from the pope, cited Cyprian's Letter to Rogatian (Letter III), in which he had stated that Christ appointed the Apostles, that is the bishops,[3] a reference which was cited also by the bishop of Città di Castella on 28 November.[4] This latter prelate granted that the Petrine primacy was accepted by Cyprian *tamquam in origine unitatis ecclesiae*; and offered an exegesis of the phrase *cujus a singulis pars in solidum tenetur*. He concentrated attention on *in solidum*, which implied at least two persons, and on *tenetur*, which must be understood of different ways of holding, since the same thing could not be held *in solidum* in the same way by several persons. He therefore expounded the phrase as allowing for the *plenitudo potestatis* of the papacy on the one hand and the *pars sollicitudinis* of the bishops on the other hand.[1] A further general reference to Letter III was made by the bishop of Gaudix on 1 December, and the bishop of Évreux quoted from Letter LXVI that Christ said to the Apostles, and thereby to all governors succeeding them, the words 'whoso heareth you, heareth Me'.[2] Similarly the bishop of Pamplona cited *De Ecclesiae Unitate* in support of his contention that since all the Apostles were equal in power so *jure divino* all bishops were equal, and that Cyprian had deduced from this that an equal and identical episcopate was bequeathed to all their successors.[3] With slight variation the bishop of Amiens also cited Letter LXVI to the effect that all Christians are the Church, which 'is made up of a people united to their bishop and a flock adhering to their pastor. Whence you should understand that the bishop is in the church, and the church in the bishop; and they who are not with the bishop, are not in the church; for the catholic church is connected together by the cement of the bishops adhering to each other.' He further quoted the phrase from *De Ecclesiae Unitate*: *episcopatus unus*, *cujus a singulis pars in solidum tenetur*, and also cited Letter XLV.[4] On 18 January 1563 the bishop of Lavaux returned to the attack, invoking Cyprian's *De Unitate* and Letter VIII in support of the contention that the residence of bishops was *jure divino*;[5] and on 12 May the cardinal of Lorraine, whilst admitting the necessity of one head of the Church, qualified this by referring to Cyprian's affirmation that *unus episcopatus est*.[1] At considerably greater length the bishop of Astorga on 9 December developed the threefold position from Cyprian: that the primacy was given to Peter; that Christ bestowed equal power on all the Apostles; and that the expansion of the Church necessitated an imparity of jurisdiction and a superiority of one head. He interpreted the phrase *cujus a singulis in solidum pars tenetur* by the analogy of many sureties, who constitute themselves such individually and severally.[2]

On the other side, the General of the Carmelites argued on 2 November for the papal *plenitudo potestatis*, and interpreted Cyprian's words *pari consortio honoris et potestatis* as referring to order and dignity of consecration, but not to administration and jurisdiction.[3] On 5 November the bishop of Cava likewise contended that order and jurisdiction were two disparate elements of the episcopal office, that Cyprian must be understood of the former only, and that whereas the Apostles received authority immediately from Christ, the bishops as their successors received it mediately through the pope.[4] Similarly the bishop of Chioggia cited chapter v of *De Unitate* as evidence that the episcopate sprang from the papacy as from a fount and the bishops were as rills therefrom.[5] The bishop of Salamanca on 30 November in supporting the plenitude of papal authority, cited chapter IV of *De Unitate*, where Cyprian quoted the Petrine texts from Matthew xvi.

18–19; and on 7 December the Abbot-General of the Cistercians appealed to Cyprian's warnings against heresies arising from breach of the unity of the Church, which unity he found in the papal supremacy.[1]

During the course of these conciliar debates the edition of Cyprian by Manutius, containing the Primacy Text, was published at Rome; and the bishop of Vintimiglia, Carlo Visconti, received at Trent letters informing him of the publication and also of the protest of Latini against the inclusion of the interpolations relating to the Petrine primacy which he had rejected. Fearing the possible effect of this disclosure on the council, Visconti consulted the bishop of Lerida, Monsignor Agostino, who confirmed the report and informed him that he had apprised Cardinal Simoneta of the facts. Accordingly on 21 June 1563 Visconti advised Rome that Latini's criticism should be discredited by authenticating the controverted passages through the testimony and approval of persons who had seen and confronted the ancient codices.[2] As a result of the division of opinion within the council, however, no definition of the relationship of the episcopate to the papacy was issued.

When the next general council of the Roman Church met in 1870, it was to be expected that Cyprian would enjoy an even greater prominence than at Trent, for the Vatican Council had before it a schema defining both the papal magisterium and papal infallibility. Appeals to the authority and words of Cyprian indeed were so many and repeated as to provoke in one of the concluding sessions, on 2 July, murmurs from several bishops *Tam saepe de Cypriano dictum est*, and even a rebuke to the bishop of Sinigaglia from the president, Cardinal de Luca, *Satis dictum est de sancto Cypriano et de sancto Augustino*.[1] In the general debate on *Pastor Aeternus*, Cardinal Constantine, bishop of Porto et Salva Candida, on 14 May contended for the Petrine primacy by appealing to Cyprian's statement that Peter received the keys before all the other Apostles; and he was followed by the bishop of Pesti who supported papal infallibility as being clearly evidenced in the early centuries, as for example by Cyprian's reference to the chair of Peter as *veritatis domicilium*.[2] On 19 May Cardinal Morenus, archbishop of Valladolid, quoted the Primacy Text of *De Unitate*, that 'he who deserts the chair of Peter, on which the church is founded, may not trust that he is in the church';[3] and on 21 May the archbishop of Cashel, replying to his brother of Tuam who had alleged the controversy between Cyprian and Stephen as proof that the former did not believe in the infallibility of the pope as teacher, argued that the matter was one of discipline, not of doctrine, in which Cyprian believed himself justified in holding to the tradition of his own Church; and therefore *causa Cypriani nihil est ad rem*.[4] Following him, the bishop of Castellammare maintained that the pope was the infallible teacher of the Church, by appealing to Cyprian's illustration of the sun and its rays, the tree and its branches, and the fountain and its rills.[1] The archbishop of Baltimore on 30 May held that the episode of Cyprian and Stephen merely demonstrated that Cyprian was in error, which he had either retracted or had purged by his martyrdom;[2] whilst the abbot of St Paul de Urbe in a written speech cited Cyprian's Letter LIX on the origin of heresies through lack of obedience to the bishop and to the principle that there is but one bishop in the Church and one judge in Christ's stead.[3]

On the other side, on 18 May, Cardinal Rauscher, archbishop of Vienna, appealed to the authority of St Augustine, who excused Cyprian's conduct towards Stephen on the ground that the universal judgement of the Church had not been pronounced on the issue; whilst the archbishop of Tuam on 20 May pointed out that Cyprian, notwithstanding his defence of unity in the Church, had withstood Stephen and had shown thereby that he did not hold the opinion of papal infallibility.[4] On 28 May the bishop of S. Augustin launched a thoroughgoing attack on the schema from Scripture and the Fathers, particularly Cyprian, using his controversy with Stephen as evidence that there was no doctrine in his time of papal infallibility, since notwithstanding his resistance Cyprian was regarded as a saint and his name occurred in the Canon of the Mass.[5] The archbishop of Halifax on 31 May examined three patristic interpretations of the Petrine text in Matthew xvi. 18–19, and argued that its application to the faith of Peter was that of the majority, the weightiest and most ancient Fathers, that several others understood it of Christ himself, whilst comparatively few interpreted it of Peter himself. In support of his contention he quoted Cyprian, Letter XXXIII, c. 1, where the author, after citing the Matthean passage, went on to declare that the Church was founded on the bishops. The archbishop affirmed that this was the very antithesis of the schema, which held that the Church was founded upon Peter alone; and proclaimed his own agreement with the general interpretation of antiquity, as evidenced by Cyprian, Origen and Chrysostom; and further he supported this by the phrase from chapter IV of *De Unitate*: *episcopatus, ut ait sanctus Cyprianus, unus est essentialiter, cujus a singulis in solidum pars tenetur.*[1]

But the most thorough exposition of the testimony of Cyprian was given in a lengthy speech on 2 June by Bishop Strossmayer of Bosnia, who insisted that no separation of the papacy from the episcopate could be justified by patristic evidence, of which he regarded Cyprian as the most authoritative exponent, both in theory and practice.[2] The Cyprianic view of the Church combined unity with respect for the rights of individual bishops and their churches, so that everything absolutist was excluded. Cyprian indeed had expounded the Petrine passages in Matthew xvi and John xx with full recognition of the unity of the Church; but having written most clearly of the Petrine primacy, he had added the rider *hoc erant utique et caeteri apostoli quod fuit Petrus, pari consortio praediti et honoris et potestatis*; and further—

(according even to the Primacy Text)—had associated the other Apostles with Peter in the office of feeding the flock, so that the universal church was one flock, tended by the unanimous consent of all the Apostles. Nor, as Strossmayer argued, could this be admitted of the Apostles and yet denied of the bishops, as if they were not successors to all the dignity and authority of the Apostles, and as if the pope alone were the successor of Peter and inheritor of his plenitude of power. Instead Cyprian had written of the unity of the episcopate, *cujus a singulis in solidum pars tenetur*; and Gregory of Nyssa had described Cyprian's authority and influence as supreme, not only in the African Church but throughout the whole of the west. Moreover, the theme of *De Unitate* was confirmed by Cyprian's action in his controversy with Stephen, which could be regarded as 'a commentary on his book', and the crux of which was a matter of faith, not of discipline. Furthermore, the testimony of Irenaeus, Tertullian and Vincent of Lérins could be adduced in support of Cyprian; and Strossmayer affirmed that the episcopate could never renounce their rights without imperilling the authority and freedom of general councils.[1] In a written speech the archbishop of St Louis also appealed to *De Unitate* in support of his argument for the corporate authority of the episcopate as successors of the apostolic college.[2]

With the closure of the introductory discussion on 4 June, and the series of detailed debates on the several chapters of the schema, inevitably much repetition occurred in regard to the citation of Cyprian. The bishop of Gurk, in support of the papal definition on 6 June, quoted chapter VI of *De Unitate*, where Cyprian, after writing of the unity of the Godhead, continued: 'and can anyone believe that this unity, which originates in the immutability of God and coheres in the heavenly mysteries, can be broken in the church and split by the divorce of clashing wills?' Again, he appealed to Cyprian's comparison in chapter VII of the seamless coat of Christ with the unity of the Church, and argued therefrom for the primacy of the chair of Peter.[1] Similarly the bishop of Concepción de Chile on 10 June rebutted the argument drawn from Cyprian that the unity of the episcopate, which the bishop held to be one of order only, conflicted with papal prerogatives.[2] The bishop of M. Varadinum on the following day cited Cyprian's words *etsi pastores multi sunt, grex tamen unus est*, as proof of the papal primacy, and the bishop of Saluzzo argued from Cyprian, Letter LV that Decius' action in preventing the election of a successor to Pope Fabian was evidence of the equation of papal power in the Church with that of the emperor in the State in the eyes of unbelievers.[3] In a speech of considerable length the abbot of St Paul de Urbe first cited Cyprian, Letter LXVI that the Church consists of 'a people united to their bishop and a flock adhering to their pastor', and also Letter XXXIII, which he interpreted to mean that as the Church was founded on the episcopate, so the episcopate was founded on Peter. Passing to *De Unitate*, he adduced the Primacy Text, particularly *et primatus Petro datur, ut una Christi ecclesia et cathedra una monstretur*; and also Letter XLVIII with its reference to Rome as *ecclesiae catholicae matricem et radicem*.[1] Similarly the bishop of Bolina appealed to Letter LVIII as evidence that heresies arose *ex defectu hujus unitatis per subordinationem supremae potestati*.[2] The patriarch of Alexandria on 20 June reverted to Cyprian's resistance to Stephen, which he dismissed as a question of discipline, and set against it the *testimonia splendida* in Cyprian's works to the supreme authority of the pope; and the archbishop-bishop of Osimo et Cingoli on 22 June cited the Primacy Text, *Et primatus datur Petro*.[3]

On the other side Cardinal Rauscher, archbishop of Vienna, appealed to the Textus Receptus of *De Unitate* in behalf of the collective responsibility of the episcopate; the archbishop of Rheims to the authority attaching to Cyprian whose name occurred in the Canon of the Mass; the bishop of Biella to Cyprian's advocacy of the status of the episcopate, and the bishop of S. Augustin to the same effect.[4] The bishops of Brieux and of Châlons-sur-Marne urged the authority of Tertullian, Cyprian, Irenaeus, and Augustine as knowing nothing either of a papal magisterium or infallibility as stated in the schema, followed by the bishop of Elna; whilst the further exposition by the bishop of Sinigaglia of the controversy between Cyprian and Stephen and of Augustine's comment thereon, led to the murmurs of dissent, *haec est mera repetitio*.[1] In the conciliar definition as finally promulged there was no citation from Cyprian; but if his name did not occur in *Pastor Aeternus*, his ghost had troubled the debates sufficiently to merit indirect reference in its phrases. For chapter I affirmed that 'the primacy of jurisdiction over the universal Church of God was immediately and directly promised and given to Blessed Peter the Apostle by Christ the Lord. For it was to Simon alone' that the Petrine passages in Matthew xvi were addressed, and likewise 'upon Simon alone' had Christ bestowed the Johannine commission.[2] *Per contra*, it was perverse opinion to 'distort the form of government established by Christ the Lord in his Church, deny that Peter in his single person, preferably to all the other Apostles, whether taken separately or together, was endowed by Christ with a true and proper primacy of jurisdiction; or... assert that the same primacy was not bestowed immediately and directly upon Blessed Peter himself, but upon the Church, and through the Church on Peter as her Minister'. The second chapter, after affirming that the see of Rome was founded by Peter, declared that 'whosoever succeeds to Peter in this see, does by the institution of Christ himself, obtain the Primacy of Peter over the whole Church'. Chapter III defined that 'primacy over the whole world' possessed by the Roman see and pontiff, as 'a superiority of ordinary power over all other churches, and this power of jurisdiction of the Roman pontiff, which is truly episcopal, is immediate; to which all, of whatever rite and dignity, both pastors and faithful, both individually and collectively are bound, by their duty of hierarchical subordination and true obedience, to submit, not only in matters which belong to faith and morals, but also in those that appertain to the discipline and government of the church throughout the world'.[1] Accordingly no appeal from the judgement of the pope to a general council, 'as to an authority higher than that of the Roman pontiff', was allowed. Chapter IV finally declared[2] that 'the Roman Pontiff, when he speaks *ex cathedra*, that is, when in discharge of the office of Pastor and Doctor of all Christians by virtue of his supreme Apostolic authority he defines a doctrine regarding faith or morals to be held by the Universal Church, by the divine assistance promised to him in blessed Peter, is possessed of that infallibility with which the divine Redeemer willed that his church should be endowed for defining doctrine concerning faith or morals; and that therefore such definitions of the Roman Pontiff are irreformable of themselves, and not from the consent of the Church'.

In contrast to Cyprian, Irenaeus enjoyed comparatively little prominence in the debates of the Vatican Council, but his controverted passage concerning the authority of Rome was cited in the formal definition. Cardinal Constantine quoted it on 14 May in his speech for the schema, and the bishop of Castellammare on 21 May urged that Irenaeus' appeal to the tradition of the Roman Church implied papal infallibility.[3] On 23 May the patriarch of

Cilicia likewise advanced it as evidence of Irenaeus' exposition of the unity of the supreme government of the Church, whilst the archbishop of Grenoble contended that the bishops were true successors of the Apostles both in teaching and governing the Church, and that Irenaeus' reference to this succession should be understood of the whole Church.[1] The fullest exegesis of Irenaeus, however, was offered by the archbishop of Baltimore, who on 30 May appealed to *magnum illud testimonium* which all Catholics used against Protestants, which was incontrovertible and which constituted a compendium of the entire controversy. From the edition of Grabe he illustrated the Protestant interpretation, that *convenire ad* implied not agreement in opinion and unity in faith, but simply the custom by members of other churches of paying a pious visit to Rome as the imperial city.[2] The same testimony was also adduced by the bishop of Nîmes on 30 May as irrefutable evidence that Irenaeus accepted the magisterium and infallibility of the pope, since he appealed to the tradition of Rome not only as that of the oldest church, but as sufficient and supreme to confute all heretics, and thereby he set forth the supreme and irreformable nature of its dogmatic authority.[3] The bishop of Augsburg likewise cited Irenaeus in behalf of the schema on 3 June, whilst Cardinal Schwarzenberg of Prague urged that his mention of the tradition of all other apostolic churches should be remembered in consideration of the Petrine primacy, and Bishop Dupanloup of Orleans emphasised the precise phrase *potiorem seu potentiorem principalitatem.*[1] On the other hand the archbishop of Smyrna claimed Irenaeus as a firm witness to papal infallibility, whilst the bishop of Biella insisted that the Church was founded on all the Apostles who were therefore judges of truth, and the archbishop of Zara appealed to Irenaeus as an authority for the pope as the witness and depositary of apostolic traditions and the Roman Church as the witness of all apostolic churches.[2] Accordingly, in chapter II of *Pastor Aeternus*, the exposition of the perpetuation of the Petrine primacy in the Roman see was reinforced by citation of the famous passage of Irenaeus: *Hac de causa ad Romanam Ecclesiam propter potentiorem principalitatem necesse semper fuit omnem convenire Ecclesiam, hoc est eos, qui sunt undique fideles.*

In the crucial issue of the Petrine and Roman primacy, therefore, the appeal to Church history would seem to have ended in deadlock. 'The later Roman theory supposes that the Church of Rome derives all its authority from the bishop of Rome as the successor of St Peter. History inverts the relationship and shews that, as a matter of fact, the power of the bishop of Rome was built upon the power of the Church of Rome. It was originally a primacy, not of the episcopate, but of the church.'[3] Nor has historical study reached unanimity concerning the two texts of Cyprian's *De Unitate*. Although the edition of Cyprian published by Fell and Pearson at Oxford in 1682 rejected the Primacy Text, that of the Benedictine Dom Maran of St Maur in 1724 adopted it (though not intended by the original editor, Baluze), whilst the Vienna edition by Hartel in 1868 decisively rejected it. During the present century Dom Chapman and Fr Bévenot have argued against the theory of interpolation and for the Cyprianic authorship of both versions; though amongst scholars adopting this conclusion, opinion has differed concerning the priority of the two versions, some holding that Cyprian wrote the Textus Receptus first against the Carthaginian dissidents and the Primacy Text later against Novatian, and others that the Primacy Text was composed first against Novatian and the Textus Receptus afterwards when Cyprian was in controversy with Stephen of Rome. In any case Cyprian's change of mind does not suggest a particularly firm and unwavering belief in the Petrine primacy (the more especially if the Primacy Text is the earlier), and the testimony of *De Unitate* has to be correlated with the rest of his writings and with his actions. Moreover Fr Bévenot's latest suggestion that the two versions imply no change of mind on Cyprian's part, but that he toned down the Primacy Text because Rome had read too much into it,[1] would point to Cyprian's interpretation of the Petrine primacy as no more than *primus inter pares*, a standpoint far different from that of *Pastor Aeternus*.

The controversy since the Reformation between Rome and other churches concerning the Petrine primacy and the papal claims illustrates moreover with especial clarity the wider problem of the relationship between Church history and theology. Granted the authenticity of the tradition of St Peter's residence and martyrdom in Rome, the evidence of I Clement and Ignatius would point to a primacy of the Church of Rome, not of the episcopate. Moreover Peter was not the founder of the Church in Rome; and until the third century the two Apostles Peter and Paul were mentioned together in the documents and traditions of the Roman Church. The appeal to Irenaeus and Cyprian was, to say the least, inconclusive as regards papal claims. Furthermore the historian of councils, Bishop Hefele of Rottenburg, in a speech at the Vatican Council on 17 May appealed to the evidence of the Council of Chalcedon against the definition in the schema of papal infallibility. Observing that if any papal document could be held to be *ex cathedra* it was the Tome of Leo, he reminded the Council of the Vatican that it was read together with a Letter of Cyril of Alexandria at the second session at Chalcedon. Whereupon, after the assembled Fathers had seen that Leo's tome was clearly in agreement with the ancient faith and the Nicene–Constantinopolitan creeds, they exclaimed unanimously, 'This is the faith of the Fathers, we all believe this. Peter has spoken by Leo, who has piously and truly taught. Cyril also has taught, Leo and Cyril have taught the same.' Hefele drew the moral that the conciliar bishops had subjected Leo's tome to their own examination concerning its orthodoxy and had approved it when they were so satisfied. 'If this doctrine of papal infallibility had been known, they would not have dared to subject the tome of Leo to their own examination, nor to pronounce judgment upon it; but without any scrutiny they would have accepted it dutifully and humbly. Moreover the conciliar Fathers treated and received the Letters of Leo and Cyril in exactly the same way.' In the fourth session all the bishops were interrogated on oath whether they found Leo's tome conformable and consonant with the Nicene–Constantinopolitan creeds; which would not have been done had they held the doctrine of papal infallibility. 'For it was not said: "Behold the dogmatic letter of the Pope, hear it and submit to it"; but it was said: "Hear and judge of it".' Even so, not all the bishops were convinced of its orthodoxy, since some bishops of Illyria and Palestine were doubtful, and therefore at the second session at Chalcedon did not give their assent. 'Nobody said to them: "Why do you act so rashly? You are not allowed to doubt."' Thus Hefele appealed to conciliar history against the Vatican definition.[1]

The difficulties created for bishops of the minority by the definition of papal magisterium and infallibility were evident from the tardiness of some of their leaders in accepting *Pastor Aeternus*. The outbreak of the Franco-Prussian war, immediately after the adjournment of the Council, entailed indeed inevitable delays in signifying their adherence to the conciliar decrees on the part of bishops of the countries engaged in hostilities. Notwithstanding, although the definition was enacted on 18 July 1870, Cardinal Schwarzenberg, archbishop of Prague, promulgated it only in January 1871, Bishop Hefele of Rottenburg in the following April, Archbishop Haynald of Kalocsa in October 1871, and Bishop Strossmayer of Bosnia in December 1872. The form of the Constitution indeed made their acceptance more difficult. On the eve of the last General Congregation of the Council, a deputation of the minority had waited on the pope to ask for such modifications as would make it possible for them to vote 'placet' at the Public Session; namely, the omission from the definition of papal magisterium of the phrase '*quae vere episcopalis est*', and from the accompanying canon of the clause censuring those who held '*aut eum habere tantum potiores partes, non vero totam plenitudinem hujus supremae potestatis*'; and the addition to the definition of papal infallibility, after the words *munere fungens*, of the phrase '*et testimonio ecclesiarum innixus*', or alternatively, '*et mediis, quae semper in ecclesia catholica usurpata fuerunt, adhibitis*', or even '*non exclusis episcopis*'. Instead of the adoption of any of these suggestions, the decree was altered, in a direction contrary to their standpoint, by the addition of the words, '*non autem ex consensu ecclesiae*'. Truly the principles of the Primacy Text of Cyprian had prevailed over those of the Textus Receptus. Moreover, the schema *De Ecclesia*, as originally presented, had contained no definition of the papal magisterium and infallibility; and it was particularly unfortunate that all further discussion of its contents had been laid aside when the decree defining the papal prerogatives was introduced towards the end of April, in order to facilitate the passing of the new constitution. Not only was the position of the minority thereby made more difficult, but the anomaly remained of a dogmatic definition of papal magisterium and infallibility, unaccompanied by a corresponding declaration of the doctrine of the Church and the episcopate.

What may be concluded therefore of the decree of the Vatican Council from the standpoint of Church history, and in regard to the twentieth-century quest for the unity of Christendom? In his address to the International Historical Congress at Rome in 1955 Pope Pius XII, in referring to the excavations in St Peter's, declared that 'en ce qui concerne l'Apôtre Pierre et sa position dans l'Église du Christ, la preuve monumentale du séjour et de la mort de Pierre à Rome n'ait pas pour la foi catholique une importance essentielle'. Professor Merrill likewise concluded his negative examination of the same problem by remarking that 'whilst he is bound by the evidence to reject absolutely the historicity of St Peter's mission in Rome, the classicist may yet, if he be also a catholic Christian, pray with all his heart' the Collect in the Liturgy for his feast-day.[1] The student of ecclesiastical history must seek a *via media* between these two opinions. Amongst scholars not of the Roman Church, from Cuthbert Turner to Oscar Cullman, there has been evident a readiness to acknowledge the unique position of St Peter amongst the Apostles, and to accept the tradition of his residence and death at Rome. Furthermore, there may be discerned a widespread willingness to recognise as a matter of historical development the pre-eminent position of the Church of Rome as in some wise *mater et caput omnium ecclesiarum*, and therewith of a primacy of honour attaching to the bishop of that see. Nor need the Church historian scruple to deny to this historical development the title familiar in his records *Providentia divina*. But it is a far cry from the evidence of the early centuries of Church history to the dogma of the Vatican Council concerning the papal magisterium and infallibility. It is possible indeed that a future general council of the Roman Church may resume consideration of the schema *De Ecclesia*, and may promulgate a dogmatic definition concerning the Church and the episcopate which will place the papacy in due relation to the Church and bishops. But the erection of a dogma *de fide* upon so insecure a foundation of historical evidence must cause the ecclesiastical historian to enter his caveat. In view of the inadequacy of the biblical evidence and the inconclusive appeal to Irenaeus and Cyprian at the Councils of Trent and the Vatican, the conversion of the primacy of the Church of Rome into the definition of *Pastor Aeternus* must cause grave concern to all who do not share Manning's robust conviction that 'whensoever any doctrine is contained in the divine tradition of the Church, all difficulties from human history are excluded', since the Church 'is its own evidence, anterior to its history and independent of it' and therefore 'no difficulties can prevail against it'.[1] For although historical evidence cannot be wholly determinative of theological interpretation, without a sufficiency of such testimony all definitions of doctrine must be precariously based. *Omnia autem probate: quod bonum est, tenete.*

CHAPTER III

SCRIPTURE AND TRADITION AT THE REFORMATION AND SINCE

'The Bible, I say, the Bible only, is the religion of Protestants.' The aphorism of William Chillingworth was designed to reduce to its simplest and shortest terms the protracted controversy between Romanists and Protestants concerning the relative authority attaching to Scripture and oral Tradition. Sweeping aside on the one hand the opinions of Bellarmine, Baronius, the Sorbonne, the Jesuits and Dominicans, and on the other side those of Luther, Calvin, Melanchthon, the Confession of Augsburg, the Genevan Confession, the Heidelberg Catechism and the Thirty-nine Articles, Chillingworth placed in opposition to each other the decrees of the Council of Trent as the official creed of the Church of Rome and the Bible only as the credendum of Protestants. Moreover he expanded his maxim concerning the adherence of Protestants to the Bible, by affirming that 'whatsoever else they believe besides it and the plain irrefragable consequences of it, well may they hold as a matter of opinion: but as a matter of Faith and Religion, neither can they with coherence to their own grounds believe it themselves, nor require the belief of it of others, without most high and schismatical presumption. I, for my part, after a long, and (as I verily believe and hope) impartial search of the true way to eternal happiness, do profess plainly that I cannot find any rest for the sole of my foot but upon this rock only.... Traditive interpretations of Scriptures are pretended, but there are few or none to be found. No Tradition but only of Scripture can derive itself from the fountain, but may be plainly proved either to have been brought in, in such an age after Christ, or that in such an age it was not in. In a word there is no sufficient certainty but of Scripture only, for any considering man to build upon.'[1] Such was the conclusion of *The Religion of Protestants, a Safe Way to Salvation*, after a century of controversy relating to the respective degree of credit to be accorded to Scripture and Tradition.

The discussion, which attained a new importance and prominence at the Reformation, was in many respects a continuation of the theological debate which had characterised the later Middle Ages. The medieval scholastic synthesis of Scripture and the Church (itself a development and elaboration of the patristic era), had suffered severe assault after the close of the thirteenth century. During the fourteenth century indeed there had become evident an increasing dichotomy of Scripture and Tradition, from which sprang several elements of the later controversy. From the side of the canonists, the most extravagant theories concerning the pope were upheld, virtually equating his power with that of

God, whilst in other quarters the theory of a post-apostolic revelation gained widespread currency. 'The breaking asunder of that synthesis in the fourteenth century not only made the Church subservient to Scripture, or the Scripture ancillary to the Church. It furthermore threw open the door by way of a supposed superiority of the Church over Holy Writ, to the idea that the Church had her own revelation, independent of that which the Apostles had recorded in their writings.'[1] In addition, the theory of an oral tradition, transmitted by word of mouth from the Apostles and not committed to writing, made its appearance, and during the fifteenth century secured considerable acceptance, with a resultant depreciation of the authority of the written Word in relation both to the Church and to unwritten Tradition. In reaction against these tendencies there arose a school of writers who affirmed the unique authority of Scripture, so that towards the end of the Middle Ages there were in conflict 'an anti-Scriptural bias and a reassertion of the primacy of Scripture'. Rarely had orthodox theology presented such a spectacle of confusion and contradiction.

To this *mélange* the sixteenth-century humanists made their own contribution, with their appeal from the Vulgate to the original tongues of the Old and New Testaments, in which process Erasmus' Greek Testament published in 1516 constituted a notable landmark, and with their search for a pattern of reform and a principle of authority in the combined witness of the New Testament and the Fathers of the early Church. Accordingly they published editions of several of the Fathers as an integral part of their resolve to recall the Church to the standards of the early centuries of its history, namely of Jerome in 1516 and 1526, of Cyprian in 1521, of Hilary in 1523, of Irenaeus in 1526, of Ambrose in 1527 and of Augustine in 1529. Towards this ideal of the humanists to break the spell of medieval scholasticism and to restore the Church to the pattern laid down in the Bible and in the early Fathers, Luther also during the years 1509–16 was sympathetic; though the pressure of controversy after the Indulgence disputes drove him in a more radical direction. His challenge to the entire hierarchy of ecclesiastical powers, in the shape of the authority of popes and councils, resulted in his elevation of Scripture to the position of sole authority and arbiter in matters of belief. At the Leipzig disputation with Eck in 1519, he affirmed that the Word of God was above all human testimonies, that all other writings were to be judged by the Holy Scriptures which possessed the greatest authority, and that he had resolved therefore to be free from the authority of papacy, councils and similar bodies.[1] In his tract *Of the Babylonish Captivity of the Church* in the following year, he rejected the seven Sacraments of the Church on the ground that the Bible recognised only three, Baptism, Penance and the Eucharist, or to speak more accurately, one Sacrament and three sacramental signs.[2] Even more emphatically in his rejoinder to Henry VIII's *Assertio septem Sacramentorum*, he complained loudly that, whereas he himself affirmed Christ and the Gospel, his adversary replied only by the Fathers, customs and decrees; so that the royal tract relied solely on the traditions of men rather than on the Word of God, whilst his appeal was to the Word and Gospel.[1] Thus to the principle of *sola fides* as the criterion for judging the merits of the several books of the Bible, there was added that of *sola Scriptura* as the standard of belief and doctrine. There can be no doubt that for Luther, the Bible was the only rule of faith.[2]

The position of Luther's *fidus Achates*, Melanchthon, was more complex. His sympathies and ties with the humanists were closer than was the case with Luther; and he clung to the hope of reconciliation and compromise with the Church of Rome. For him the creeds of the early Church had a greater authority, though he agreed with his master that Scripture should be the source and standard of judgement of dogmas and creeds. 'We receive faithfully in our churches the Apostles', Nicene and Athanasian Creeds, and we condemn all the errors repugnant to these creeds which the Catholic Church of Christ condemned; and we recognize these creeds to be truly handed down in the Word of God written by Prophets and Apostles.' Melanchthon was always ready to listen attentively to the *Ecclesia docens et admonens*, and likewise to regard the Fathers as *testes veteris et primae Ecclesiae*. He accepted the Christology expressed in the Nicene creed, and affirming 'the doctrine of Christ's Catholic Church, contained in the Prophetic and Apostolic Scriptures and in the Creeds', claimed therefore truly to be 'in accord with the Catholic Church'.[1]

Equally interesting and important were the opinions of Bucer on the authority to be attached to the tradition of the Church and the interpretations of the Fathers. In respect of the Colloquy of Ratisbon he undertook to demonstrate 'not only by the divine Scriptures but also by the writings of the holy Fathers, that we adhere to no heresy but carefully follow the truly catholic agreement of the Church in all things'.[2] He insisted indeed that Scripture must be the standard and criterion of tradition, though he placed great value on tradition considered in itself, and particularly on the tradition of the primitive Church in its pristine purity, with which the Scriptures were entirely conformable. Accordingly he was much attracted by the *consensus quinquesaecularis*, and stood as a link between Erasmus and Melanchthon on the one hand and Witzel, Cassander and Calixtus on the other hand. But his regard for tradition was of both a polemical and an eirenical character. The pattern of the primitive Church served as a standard by which to measure the decline which had supervened in later ages, whilst his emphasis on the distinction between Fundamentals and Non-essentials was reinforced by his appeal to early tradition. For him *Je alter sie ist, desto wahrer ist sie.*[3] At Zürich, in succession to Zwingli who had declared that he would 'accept no one as judge and witness except the Scriptures, the Spirit of God speaking from the Scriptures', Bullinger likewise appealed to the authority of the Bible. To his *Decades* indeed he prefaced an exposition *Of the Four General Synods or Councils*, and he further allowed 'that the Lord Jesus both did and spake many things which were not written by the apostles'; but he contended that 'it followeth not therefore that the doctrine of the word of God, taught by the apostles, is not absolutely perfect'. Furthermore, 'as for those which do earnestly affirm that all points of godliness were taught by the apostles to posterity by word of mouth and not by writings, their purpose is to set to sale their own, that is, men's ordinances instead of the word of God'. He accordingly issued this challenge to the Romanists: 'Let them set forth those their traditions, which they receive as reverently as the Scripture; for then it shall easily appear, by the likeness or by the contrariety, what came from the apostles and what is privily conveyed under their names. For this is without all doubt, that the apostles of God delivered nothing by their lively word of mouth that was contrary to their writings, which they delivered afterwards to their posterity that came after them. Wherefore that cannot be apostolic at all, which is contrary to the writings of the apostles.'[1]

The rejoinders of Romanists to the advocacy of *sola Scriptura* were affected unfavourably by the circumstance that Catholic thought was 'in a ferment seldom equalled in the history of doctrine', so that 'under a common concern for the traditional doctrine of the Church, the catholics became more divided than ever in their formulation of the relation of Scripture to the Church'.[1] All apologists concurred in emphasising the insufficiency of Scripture alone, on the dual grounds that the Bible itself was often obscure and needing interpretation and that there were several doctrines of the Catholic faith not explicitly contained in Scripture; so that the authority of the Church was necessary, both to offer a clear and authentic exposition of doubtful passages in the Bible, and also to supply deficiencies in its record by virtue of the further source of revelation committed to the keeping of the Church in the shape of oral tradition. But there were differences of opinion concerning their respective status. Eck, for example, starting from 'the superiority of Scripture over the Church', ended 'at the opposite pole, superiority of the Church over Scripture', having accepted meanwhile 'the idea of an apostolic tradition outside Scripture'.[2] Cochlaeus defended the authority of the Church, as being itself the authenticator and interpreter of Scripture and also as teaching from its own tradition many things not contained in Scripture. Similarly Driedo emphasised the function of the Church as expositor of the written Word, in discharging which office it brought out of its treasure-store things new and old; so that even doctrines not explicitly or implicitly indicated in Scripture but satisfying the conditions of the

Vincentian canon, were to be received as having been transmitted by the Apostles. To Pighius, the pupil of Driedo, the two principles upon which Christian belief was built were canonical Scripture and unwritten ecclesiastical Tradition outside Scripture; and of these two, Tradition was superior, since it embraced Scripture as one of its constituents. Whilst a distinction was made between doctrinal traditions and those relating to customs and ceremonies, the tendency was becoming evident to reply to the maxim of *sola Scriptura* by that of *propter Ecclesiam solam*.

Against this background of confused, and to some extent contradictory, theological discussion must be set the decree of the Council of Trent at its fourth session on 8 April 1546, defining the authority attaching respectively to Scripture and Tradition, in the following terms:

The Holy, Oecumenical and General Synod of Trent... having this aim always before its eyes, that errors may be removed and the purity of the Gospel be preserved in the Church, which was before promised through the prophets and which our Lord Jesus Christ, the Son of God, first published with his own mouth and then commanded to be preached through his Apostles to every creature, as the source of all saving truth and of discipline of conduct; and perceiving that this truth and this discipline are contained in written books and in unwritten Traditions, which were received by the Apostles from the lips of Christ himself, or by the same Apostles at the dictation of the Holy Spirit, and were handed down and have come down to us; following the example of the orthodox Fathers, this Synod receives and venerates with equal adhesion of faith and reverence all the books both of the New and Old Testaments, since one God is the author of both, together with the said Traditions, as well those pertaining to faith as those pertaining to morals, as having been given either from the lips of Christ or by the dictation of the Holy Spirit, and preserved by unbroken succession in the Church.[1]

Behind the formulation of this decree lay much debate, during which not inconsiderable differences of opinion had been evident, both as to the form and also the content of the definition. The council began by equating Scripture with the canonical books of the Bible and by considering also ecclesiastical tradition outside Scripture, and thence passed to discussion of their relationship, and whether only apostolic traditions should be mentioned in the decree. The question received a brief mention on 15 February, and was resumed on the 28th at a meeting of one of the three sections into which the council had divided itself for the despatch of business. The bishop of Fano argued that acceptance of oral tradition followed necessarily from that of the written Scriptures, since both were dictated by the Holy Spirit, and the bishop of Belcastro urged that in addition to apostolic traditions, ecclesiastical traditions and customs should be included in the decree. Cardinal de Santa Croce affirmed that the sole difference between the Scriptures and traditions lay in the circumstance that the latter had not been committed to writing; and he proceeded to lay down three principles and fundamentals of the Faith;

first, the written Scriptures, composed at the dictation of the Holy Spirit; secondly, the Gospel which Christ had committed not to writing but to the lips and hearts of his Apostles, and parts of which they had subsequently set down in writing whilst the rest remained in oral tradition; and thirdly, since Christ could not remain with us in the flesh, he had given the Holy Spirit to teach the Church all truth and to determine any doubts arising in the minds of men. After this preliminary discussion, the matter was remitted for thorough examination by a commission of theologians, whose report was received on 23 February by the section; which thereupon decided to include the Bible and Tradition in one single decree, and the subsequent debate turned on the questions of the various kinds of tradition involved and whether to specify the different traditions or simply to make a general reference to them. The bishop of Feltre was of opinion that these traditions should not be named in detail but should be stated generally, since great difficulty would arise if all the traditions should be set forth. Against this the General of the Augustinians urged that since the various traditions enjoyed different authority in the Church, they should be received in different ways. Thus those pertaining to faith should be received with the same authority as the Gospel, whilst those subject to change, as for example, concerning ceremonies, had not the same status. Cardinal Pacheco, bishop of Jaen, wished to add to the proposed definition the words: 'In addition to the Sacred

Books we have various usages in the Church, delivered to the Church by the Apostles and transmitted to us, which although not written down are observed by the authority of the Church.'

In view of the differences of opinion, the decision whether traditions should be mentioned *per genus* or *per species* was remitted to the next General Congregation on 26 February, when Cardinal de Santa Croce laid before the Council the two alternatives: *ne ita simpliciter traditiones apostolicae recipiantur*: or *ut ipsarum enumeratio a Concilio fieret*. Cardinal Pacheco favoured a general mention, since specification would be dangerous; the archbishop of Torre wished to include all ecclesiastical traditions in general, lest if apostolic traditions alone were mentioned, the rest might seem to be rejected; and the turbulent bishop of Chioggia, the Dominican Nacchianti, took the extreme position of advocating the omission even of apostolical traditions, whilst refusing in any wise to countenance the mention of ecclesiastical traditions, some of which, he affirmed, were a burden to the faithful. The bishop of Bertinoro wished apostolical traditions to be placed on the same basis as the Scriptures, and Cardinal Pole emphasised that the abuses of various traditions threatened the discipline of the Church. In view of the continuing diversity of opinion, the President proposed that the drafting of a decree joining the Scriptures with tradition should be entrusted to a committee of the bishops.

On 22 March the text of the proposed decree was

circulated, declaring that those traditions, whether delivered orally by Christ himself or by the Holy Spirit, and preserved in the Catholic Church by a continuous succession, should be received and venerated by all faithful Christians with equal adhesion of faith and with the highest reverence; and thereby containing the controversial phrase *par pietatis affectus*, *summa cum reverentia*. When this definition was considered by the appropriate section on the following day, the bishop of Sinigaglia advocated a form of words defining true apostolic traditions, lest a general acceptance of traditions should include some which had been abolished. In order to meet this point, the bishop of Feltre proposed that the decree should include the words *traditiones*, *quae successive usque ad nos pervenerint*, and the bishop of Belcastro emphasised this point. The bishop of Feltre further suggested the substitution of the words: *quas* [*traditiones*] *quidem colere pari debemus affectu*, and the bishop of Sinigaglia again pressed for the traditions to be defined; whilst the bishop of Castellammare urged that in addition to apostolic traditions, there should be included ecclesiastical traditions relating to divine worship. The bishop of Fano, however, protested that the phrase *pari pietatis affectu* was untrue, since traditions, although inspired by the Holy Spirit, were variable, whilst Scripture was unchanging; to which the bishop of Belcastro retorted that since both sources of faith were from the same author, they should be received with the same authority, and the fact that certain traditions were variable was likewise due to the inspiration of the Holy Spirit; whereupon the bishop of Feltre intervened again to emphasise the important difference between apostolic and ecclesiastical traditions. The discussion was continued in the General Congregation on 27 March, when the bishop of Sinigaglia suggested that either the apostolic traditions should be enumerated or else all mention of traditions should be omitted. The bishop of Fano returned to his contention that Scripture and traditions could not be received *pari pietatis affectu*, since there was the greatest difference between them, inasmuch as the former was unvarying and the latter were variable according to the decision of the Church. Moreover, he added, if the council adopted a decree which accepted oral tradition as a source of dogma, it would be a direct assault on the Lutheran position; and he proposed a milder variant form of words: 'since this Holy Synod is aware that many other things in the Church are dictated by the Holy Spirit, which are not set forth in the sacred writings, therefore it receives and reverences these also.' In support of his contention he remarked that certain apostolical traditions, such as communion in both kinds, standing for prayer between Easter and Whitsun, and turning to the east when praying, had been altered by the Church, whilst others had fallen into desuetude by the negligence and carelessness of the Church. This criticism provoked a reply from the bishop of Bitonto, defending the phrase in question and pointing out that some undoubtedly apostolic rules, such as those of the Council of Jerusalem concerning things strangled, were of temporary duration and had properly fallen into desuetude. The bishop of Worcester opposed *pari pietatis affectu*, also on the ground that traditions could be observed, altered or abolished according to the determination of the Church, whereas the Scriptures had never been changed or abolished. Finally it was resolved to lay three questions before the Fathers at a proximate General Congregation, upon which they should vote *placet* or *non placet*.

These questions were accordingly circulated: first, whether it was sufficient that the decree should specify apostolic traditions as existing in the Church, or whether it should be required that they should be received as such; secondly, whether the phrase *pari pietatis affectu* should be retained, or whether some other form of words, expressive of the due reverence to be accorded to such traditions, ought to be substituted therefor; and thirdly, whether, if the phrase were retained, there should be added some further words expressing the parity to be given to traditions pertaining to dogmas of the faith as to doctrines contained in Scripture, and whether a distinction should be made in respect of traditions pertaining to morals. Upon the submission of the matter to the bishops, forty-four votes were cast for the reception of apostolic traditions, and seven for their mention only, with one prelate *dubius*; for *pari pietatis affectu* there voted thirty-three bishops, for *similis pietatis affectus* eleven, for *reverentia debita* three, whilst three were *dubii*, and two voted *non placet* to any formula; furthermore thirteen favoured the equation of traditions concerning both faith and morals, eleven voted in a contrary direction and for a difference between those relating to morals and to faith, and *alii non curarunt*. When the General Congregation considered these answers on 5 April, the bishop of Sinigaglia voiced his regret that whereas the decree mentioned only those traditions which had persisted to his own time, traditions which had fallen into desuetude and ought to be revived, were not mentioned; and the bishops of Castellammare and Fano urged once more the reconsideration of *pari pietatis affectu*. The bishops of Bitonto and of Bertinoro defended the phrase, and the bishop of Astorga wished ecclesiastical traditions also to be included. The bishop of Bergamo agreed with his brother of Sinigaglia, and further proposed the substitution of *simili pietate* for *pari pietatis affectu*. The bishop of Chioggia forthrightly denounced the equation of oral tradition with Scripture as *impium*, an aspersion which moved Cardinal Pacheco and the bishop of Bertinoro to indignant protest, the latter exclaiming *Hoc dicere haeresis est*. Bishop Nacchianti, however, repeated his opinion that it was impious to equate the Gospel according to St John with the apostolic tradition of turning towards the east in prayer; and when asked by Cardinal de Santa Croce whether he received the tradition of the Canon of the Mass with equal piety as the sacred books, he replied *Sic, ut Evangelium*. After further pointed exchanges, in which Cardinals

Madruzzo, Pole and Del Monte reprobated the use of *impium*, the bishop of Chioggia (though not recanting his opinion) expressed his regret that he had given offence to the Council, whereupon shouts were raised for his pardon, and Cardinal Del Monte as President made the sign of the cross in blessing over him. When the discussion was resumed in the meeting of the section, it was agreed that the phrase *pari pietatis affectu* should stand, since it represented the wish of a majority. The bishop of Belcastro made a last attempt to secure mention in the decree of ecclesiastical traditions, but was opposed by Cardinal de Santa Croce, who further pointed out that the restriction of traditions to those *quae ad nos pervenerint* excluded by implication *aliae quae non pervenerunt*.

In the Fourth Session of the Council on 8 April, therefore, the decree was formally adopted, the bishop of Chioggia saying only the single word *Obediam*. In its final form the definition represented an evident compromise between the desire of some bishops for the inclusion of ecclesiastical traditions along with apostolic, and the reluctance of others to ascribe an identity of authority to oral traditions, even though apostolic, and the written Word. The decree avoided any dichotomy of Scripture and Tradition by affirming that the truth of the Gospel, both in belief and conduct, was 'contained in written books and in unwritten traditions'. Furthermore, the traditions were restricted to 'those pertaining to faith and to morals', thereby excluding ecclesiastical customs and ceremonies. Both Scripture and Traditions were declared to have been 'received by the Apostles from the lips of Christ himself, or by the same Apostles at the dictation of the Holy Spirit and were handed down and have come down to us'; and the Traditions were such as had 'been given either from the lips of Christ himself or by the dictation of the Holy Spirit, and preserved by unbroken succession in the Church'. With these safeguards the Council received 'with equal adhesion of faith and reverence' both Scripture and the Traditions, 'as well those pertaining to faith as those pertaining to morals'. This Janus-like character of the definition involved both Romanists and Protestants in a situation of equal delicacy and difficulty. For the acceptance of such traditions only as were of direct provenance from the Apostles and had been handed down in unbroken succession in the Church, imposed upon apologists the task of demonstrating both their apostolic origin and their uninterrupted transmission; whilst the equation of oral tradition with Scripture as the basis of dogma presented the retort courteous, if not also the lie direct, to the Protestant assertion of the sole authority of the Bible in matters of doctrine. In a considerable measure the decree elevated the testimony of ecclesiastical history into a court of appeal in respect of dogmas, since historical evidence was necessary to establish their apostolic origin and unbroken succession in the Church. Neither Protestants nor Romanists however, being ignorant of the debates which had preceded the definition, were aware at once of all its implications nor of the precise significance of its phrases, and the controversy therefore continued for some time to move in its accustomed channels.

To so direct and forthright a challenge the Protestants were bound to make reply; and the *Examinis Concilii Tridentini Opus Integrum, Quatuor Partes* of Martin Chemnitz, published at Frankfort in 1565–73, did so to the extent of 800 double-column, folio pages. In dealing with the decree concerning Tradition, Chemnitz declared it to be a veritable Pandora's box (*vere est Pandorae pyxis*), from which any doctrine or usage of the Roman Church could be produced, and, since no scriptural proof was required, could be affirmed to be an apostolic tradition. Moreover, since 'tradition' itself was a portmanteau-word, he distinguished eight different kinds of tradition, which he proceeded to examine seriatim. The first kind consisted of things which Christ and his Apostles had transmitted orally and which had been subsequently committed to writing by the Apostles and Evangelists. Such, for example, was the baptismal formula; and he noted further that Cyprian had traced the mingling of water with wine in the Eucharistic chalice to Dominical tradition. Traditions of this nature which were consonant with the written Scriptures, Chemnitz was therefore prepared to accept, and justified his attitude by an appeal to Irenaeus' statements concerning Polycarp (as reported by Eusebius); namely that 'he constantly taught those things which he had learned from the Apostles, which also are the tradition of the church, which alone are true'; that at Rome he converted many heretics by 'preaching that the one and only truth which he had received from the Apostles, was that which is the tradition of the church'; and that in his recollections of the teaching of the Apostles, he 'reported all things in agreement with the Scriptures'. The touchstone of traditions for Chemnitz therefore was that, in accordance with Polycarp's teaching, they should be πάντα σύμφωνα ταῖς γραφαῖς.[1]

The second kind of tradition was that the books of Holy Scripture, having been guarded by the Church and faithfully transmitted to posterity, have been handed down to us in an uninterrupted sequence of time and by a sure succession. Thus, for example, Origen said that by tradition (ἐν παραδόσει) he had learned that the four Gospels were universally received by the Church, and Eusebius appealed to the authority of the Church in regard to disputed books in the Canon of Scripture. This genus of tradition therefore Chemnitz reverently received, since by it the Church confessed itself bound to doctrine consonant with Scripture and thereby bound posterity likewise to such doctrine. In so doing, he contrasted the appeal of the Fathers to the agreement of tradition with Scripture with the claim of the Roman Church of his own day to base its doctrines and customs on unwritten tradition alone.[2] The third kind of tradition specified by Chemnitz was that urged against heretics by Irenaeus in chapters 3 and 4 of Book III of his *Adversus Haereses* and by Tertullian in *De Praescriptione Haereticorum*. For Irenaeus, in reply to the heretics' claim to possess a secret tradition, appealed to the authentic tradition handed down in churches descended from the Apostles, whilst Tertullian similarly affirmed that 'we are in communion with the apostolic churches because there is no difference of doctrine', whereas heretics set forth a teaching which, 'when compared with that of the Apostles, will proclaim by its diversity and contrariety that it originates neither from an apostle nor from an apostolic man'. Therefore, Chemnitz concluded, these early writers 'proved by tradition the truth, authority and sufficiency of Scripture, because the dogmas of faith were the same as those contained in Scripture and those received by the primitive Church from the Apostles' tradition, and faithfully preserved until their own time. For not a single point in the entire argument of Irenaeus and Tertullian can be shown relating to any doctrine which they produced from tradition alone, and which could not be proved by any testimony of Scripture.'[1] Accordingly, Chemnitz accepted the three creeds as true and ancient traditions of the Apostles.

In support of his fourth kind of tradition, namely that of exposition of the true sense and meaning of Scripture, he appealed again to Irenaeus and Tertullian as having discharged this task against the falsely pretended traditions of heretics. 'For there is no doubt that the primitive Church received from the Apostles and apostolic men, not only the text (so to speak) of Scripture, but also its legitimate and native interpretation'; and 'these genuine, ancient and true apostolic traditions', Chemnitz added, 'we receive with the highest reverence'.[1] A fifth kind of tradition was that of dogmas which, though not contained in the express words and syllables of Scripture, had been deduced by the Fathers by good, sure, firm and clear process of reasoning from the manifest evidence of the Bible.[2] Such, for example, were the Deity of the Holy Spirit, the custom of infant baptism and the decision that heretical baptism should not be repeated, the Nicene use of *homoousion* and the doctrine of the two Natures of Christ. Closely allied to this was the sixth kind of tradition, namely 'that which is ascribed to the universal consensus of the Fathers: for this form of words is used: "The Fathers have thus handed down."' Indubitably Protestants gave to the writings of the Fathers such honourable place as was their due; 'for it is our opinion that in controversies concerning religion, the judge should be the Word of God, and that afterwards should come the confession of the true Church'.[3]

In regard to the Fathers, therefore, Chemnitz defined his seventh kind of tradition by affirming that when 'the Fathers make reference to non-Scriptural traditions, they do not properly understand dogmas of faith which ought to be received without Scripture, or outside and beyond Scripture, as though they need not be proved by any evidence of Scripture; but they speak of certain ancient rites and usages, which on account of their antiquity are referred to the Apostles'. Such customs were the use of the sign of the cross, turning to the east in prayer, the *epiklesis* in the Eucharist, the blessing of the baptismal font, threefold immersion at baptism and the renunciation of Satan, and kneeling during prayer. Chemnitz contended, therefore, that when the Fathers spoke of oral traditions, they referred to such things and not to doctrines of faith; and that a distinction should accordingly be made between *credenda* on the one hand and rites and ceremonies on the other hand. 'For if agreement has been previously reached concerning doctrine, concord and regulation can easily be achieved concerning rites.'[1] It was evident indeed from the testimony of Scripture that the Apostles had ordained certain rites which they had handed down to their churches, and probability also indicated that they had established others, not mentioned in the Bible; and the Church had continued this practice. Chemnitz, therefore, laid down certain standards by which to test these rites and ceremonies. First, some could plead an indirect authorisation by Scripture; such as the rules for propriety in celebrating the Lord's Supper, for the separation and excommunication of disorderly walkers, and for the appointment of ministers. Further examples were the various ceremonies attaching to the rite of baptism, which were illustrative and explicative of its doctrine. All such usages were to be approved. Secondly came rules concordant with the apostolic precept that all things should be done decently and in order; such, for example, as the regulation that women should be covered in church, or for the subordination of spiritual gifts to the common edification, and other similar rules for preserving good order in the public assemblies of the Church. All such things, 'which (as has been elegantly said) are inducements and bonds of piety', should be retained. Thirdly, the principle in all such matters should be that of Christian liberty; for since ceremonies are in their nature *adiaphora*, they should be few, useful and such as tend to edification: and it should be recognised that they can be altered, abrogated and instituted according to varying circumstances. Chemnitz's rule in such matters was that *doctrina... universalis et perpetua est*, *ritus vero pro circumstantiis mutari libere possunt*; and from this it followed that, whilst not rejecting all such traditions, there was little profit in disputation as to which had descended from the Apostles and at what time and in what place.

Seven kinds of tradition therefore were accepted by Chemnitz; and only the eighth was to be rejected, namely, that in current controversy between Roman Catholics and Protestants concerning traditions, pertaining both to faith and to morals, which could not be proved by any testimony of Scripture, but which nevertheless the Council of Trent had required to be received with equal adhesion of faith and reverence. Moreover, Chemnitz cited Peter Soto as interpreting this decree in the sense that 'it is a catholic and infallible rule that whatsoever the Roman church believes, holds and uses, although not contained in Scripture, is handed down from the Apostles; even if the beginning of such observances, their author and origin are unknown nor can be ascertained, yet they are undoubtedly derived from the Apostles'. Amongst such traditions, Soto specified the offering of the sacrifice of the altar, the anointing with chrism, invocation of saints, meritorious works, the papal primacy, the blessing of the water at baptism, Confirmation, the elements, words and effects of the Sacraments of Order, Matrimony and Extreme Unction, prayers for the dead, and the detailed enumeration of sins to the priest in confession with the necessity of satisfaction. All these, in the opinion of Chemnitz, were not *adiaphora*, but were very important matters. In conclusion, therefore, he summarised comprehensively his own position in regard to Tradition. 'We do not simply reject all traditions which the ancients celebrated under that title and name. Those contained in or consonant with Scripture, we do not disapprove. But the question chiefly concerns those traditions which cannot be proved by any testimony of Scripture. In regard to these, it is not sufficient simply to assert that there is an apostolic tradition; ... nor does it suffice if one of the Fathers has said that this tradition derives from the apostles.' More particularly, there was a clear distinction between matters of doctrine and of rites. For dogmas of faith, scriptural authority was essential. For rites and ceremonies 'those rites which are consonant with Scripture, are rightly to be retained; those contrary to Scripture should justly and without rashness be rejected and abolished. But if the question concerns adiaphoristic rites, not contrary to Scripture, ...if they are not set forth as matters of necessity, of worship and merit, but merely as serving order, decency and edification, and if they are not contrary to Christian liberty, then order may be made concerning them as seems good to the Church for edification.'[1]

Writing from the Lutheran standpoint Chemnitz might well have appeared ready to go seven-eighths of the way with his Roman Catholic adversaries. Moreover, he believed that the emphasis laid upon apostolic traditions by the Tridentine decree had changed the course of controversy between Romanists and Protestants. During the earlier phases of the dispute with Luther, he discerned a dominant tendency on the part of Romanists to rely upon the authority and pronouncements of the Church itself. 'That which the Church decreed, should have equal force and authority with those things which were clearly set forth in the Scriptures by divine authority.' Since the decree of the Council of Trent, however, he averred that the ground had been shifted to unwritten apostolic traditions; and as a result the question became to a considerable extent one of Church history, since historical evidence must be sought to prove the antiquity of such traditions as were affirmed to be of apostolic provenance, as he illustrated in respect of clerical celibacy, believing that much light could be thrown on this particular controversy *ex historica consuetudine.*

But if Chemnitz had shown a generous disposition to go two miles with his adversary, Calvin was less inclined to venture even one mile with Roman controversialists. In the definitive edition of the *Institutes* in 1559, he made plain his position. In the preface addressed to the king of France, he referred to 'the true religion which is handed down in the Scriptures', and contrasted it with the Romanists' emphasis on the Mass, Purgatory, and pilgrimages, 'since they can prove none of these by the Word of God'. Furthermore in respect of their appeal to the consensus of the Fathers, he affirmed 'that by their authority...the better part of the victory (to speak with great modesty) would belong to us'; and he repudiated the suggestion that Protestants were 'despisers and adversaries of the Fathers'.[1] In the First Book, *Of the Knowledge of God the Creator*, Calvin animadverted on 'the most pernicious error...that the Scriptures have only such weight as is conceded to them by the suffrages of the Church', and insisted in refutation 'that Scripture is self-authenticated, carrying its own evidence along with it, and ought not to submit to proofs and arguments, but obtains the conviction which it merits with us by the testimony of the Spirit'. He allowed, however, that 'for the best of reasons, the consent of the Church is not without its weight; for it is not to be accounted of no consequence that, from the first publication of Scripture, so many ages have uniformly concurred in yielding obedience to it'.[1]

The fullest exposition of his standpoint in regard to the respective authority of the Church and of Tradition, is contained in the Fourth Book *Of the Holy, Catholic Church*. 'Let this then be a sure axiom—that nothing ought to be admitted in the Church as the Word of God save that which is contained, first in the Law and the Prophets, and secondly, in the writings of the Apostles; and that there is no other method of teaching in the Church than according to the prescription and rule of his Word.' Even the Apostles had no other function 'than was formerly permitted to the prophets, namely to expound the ancient Scriptures and show that the things there delivered, are fulfilled in Christ'; and in his promise to them of the gift of the Holy Spirit, the restriction which Christ imposed was to be noted: he assigns to the Holy Spirit this office 'to bring to remembrance what his own lips had previously taught'. There was, moreover, 'this difference between the Apostles and their successors, that they were sure and authentic amanuenses of the Holy Spirit and therefore their writings are to be regarded as the oracles of God, whereas others have no other office than to teach what is delivered and sealed in the holy Scriptures'. Indeed precisely at this point Calvin discerned the *differentia* between Romanist and Protestant. 'This therefore is the difference. They ascribe an authority to the Church independent of the Word of God; we however wish it to be annexed to the Word and will not suffer it to be separated from it.' If his adversaries argued that 'it was necessary for the Church to add some things to the writings of the Apostles, or for themselves to supply afterwards, orally, what they had set forth insufficiently clearly', he replied in the words of St Augustine: 'When the Lord is silent, which of us may say "These or those things are"; or if we should be bold to say it, how should we prove it?' If his opponents further brought forth the sanction given by the Council of Nicaea to the non-Scriptural term *homoousion*, 'I confess that this word does not occur in Scripture; but since it is so often asserted there that there is one God, and Christ is so often called true and eternal God, one with the Father, what are the Nicene Fathers doing when they declare him to be of the one essence, save simply to set forth the natural sense of Scripture?' As with Nicaea, so with other councils. 'Whenever the decree of any council is brought forward, I would desire first carefully to consider on what occasion it was held, for what end, and with what intention, and who were present; and then I would have the matter discussed to be examined by the rule of Scripture.' By this means Calvin believed that 'councils would enjoy their proper dignity, yet Scripture would enjoy the highest place, since nothing would be done which was not subjected to its rule. Thus the ancient Councils of Nicaea, Constantinople, the first of Ephesus, Chalcedon and the like, which were held for the confutation of errors, we willingly embrace and reverence as sacred in so far as relates to the doctrines of faith, for they contain nothing but the pure and natural interpretation of Scripture, which the holy Fathers adopted with spiritual prudence to crush the enemies of religion then arising.' The deliberate qualification—*quantum attinet ad fidei dogmata*—was of the utmost importance; for Calvin distinguished sharply between the conciliar decisions relating to dogma and the decrees concerning rites and ceremonies. The former could be brought to the sole test of conformity to Scripture; *haec enim una est certa lex discretionis*; and therefore a council was a proper means of interpreting Scripture in the formulation of doctrine, provided always that its decrees should 'set forward a definition taken out of Scripture'. But with regard to contemporary Romanist customs in controverted issues, 'of Purgatory, of the intercession of the Saints, of auricular confession and the like, not one syllable can be found in Scripture'.[1]

With regard to rites and ceremonies, Calvin stoutly 'inveighed against that tyranny of human traditions which is haughtily obtruded upon us in the name of the Church'. Equally he denied that the traditions ascribed by the Roman Church to the Apostles had been handed down from them. 'If any credit is to be given to ancient histories and records, that which is attributed to the apostles was not only unknown to them, but also unheard of by them.' Furthermore he laid down the invariable principle that all ecclesiastical regulations and ordinances should have a positive basis and precept in Scripture. 'I approve of those human institutions only which are founded upon the authority of God and derived from Scripture, and therefore are certainly divine.'[1] Throughout the *Institutes*, Calvin appealed frequently to both Greek and Latin Fathers, and especially Augustine, in support of his own position and in criticism of the contentions of the Romanists. Twenty years before the appearance of the final edition of the *Institutes*, in his *Responsio ad Sadoleti Epistolam* in 1539, he had affirmed that the consensus of antiquity was more on his own side than in favour of his opponents, and had avowed his purpose to restore 'that form of the Church which the apostles laid down, in which we have the only pattern of the true Church'. He was willing indeed to extend the period of this primitive Church to embrace the times of Basil and John Chrysostom among the Greeks, and of Cyprian, Ambrose, and Augustine amongst the Latins. But to the Fathers and Councils he would concede a certain authority only in so far as they agreed with the rule of Scripture, which alone was above question. Thus his appeal to Church history was designed as a means of testing the authenticity of Romanist claims in behalf of traditions which were set forth as apostolic, and as such was a weapon of not inconsiderable force.

Another aspect of the controversy concerning the relationship of Scripture and Tradition was reflected in the definitions of the Church of England. In the

Thirty-nine Articles of Religion, Article VI, *Of the Sufficiency of the Holy Scriptures for Salvation*, declared that 'Holy Scripture containeth all things necessary to salvation, so that whatsoever is not read therein, nor may be proved thereby, is not to be required of any man, that it should be believed as an article of the Faith or be thought requisite or necessary to salvation'. Accordingly the Three Creeds 'ought thoroughly to be received and believed, for they may be proved by most certain warrants of Holy Scripture'. Article XX, *Of the Authority of the Church*, stated that 'the Church hath power to decree Rites or Ceremonies, and authority in Controversies of Faith; And yet it is not lawful for the Church to ordain anything that is contrary to God's Word written;...Wherefore, although the Church be a witness and a keeper of Holy Writ, yet, as it ought not to decree anything against the same, so besides the same ought it not to enforce anything to be believed for necessity of salvation.' The same standard was applied in Article XXI, *Of the Authority of General Councils*; of which it was averred that 'they may err, and sometimes have erred, even in things pertaining unto God; wherefore things ordained by them as necessary to salvation have neither strength nor authority, unless it may be declared that they be taken out of Holy Scripture'. Furthermore the sixth item of the Canons of 1571 required preachers not to teach anything as necessary to be believed 'but that which is agreeable to the doctrine of the Old and New Testament, and that which the Catholic fathers and ancient bishops have collected out of that doctrine'. In his classic apologetic for the Anglican *via media*, *Of The Laws of Ecclesiastical Polity*, Hooker commented upon and expounded the meaning of these Articles. He allowed that 'it may be and oftentimes hath been demanded, how the books of Holy Scripture contain in them all necessary things, when of things necessary the very chiefest is to know what books we are bound to esteem holy, which point is confessed impossible for the Scripture itself to teach'; and in reply urged that 'necessary' cannot mean 'simply of all things which are necessary, but all things that are necessary in some certain kind or form; as all things which are necessary, and either could not at all, or could not easily, be known by the light of natural discourse; all things which are necessary to be known that we may be saved; but known with presupposal of knowledge concerning certain principles whereof it receiveth us already persuaded, and then instructeth us in all the residue that are necessary. In the number of these principles one is the sacred authority of Scripture.' Further, he agreed that the doctrines of the Trinity, of the coeternity of the Son and of the double procession of the Holy Spirit, as also the duty of paedobaptism, are 'in Scripture nowhere to be found by express literal mention, only deduced they are out of Scripture by collection'. Following the Anglican *via media*, he rejected 'two opinions...concerning sufficiency of holy Scripture, each extremely opposite unto the other and both repugnant unto truth. The schools of Rome teach Scripture to be so unsufficient, as if, except traditions were added, it did not contain all revealed and supernatural truth, which absolutely is necessary for the children of men in this life to know that they may in the next be saved. Others justly condemning this opinion, grow likewise unto a dangerous extremity, as if Scripture did not only contain all things in that kind necessary, but all things simply, and in such sort that to do anything according to any other law, were not only unnecessary but even opposite unto salvation, unlawful and sinful.' Therefore 'we hold not the Church further tied herein unto Scripture, than that against Scripture nothing be admitted in the Church'.[1]

By his recognition that 'a number of things there are for which the Scripture hath not provided by any law, but left them unto the careful discretion of the Church', Hooker was able to use tradition and reason as secondary and ancillary aids. 'We are to search how the Church in these cases may be well directed to make that provision by laws which is most convenient and fit; and what is so in these cases, partly Scripture and partly reason must teach to discern.' Traditions, therefore, must be brought to the test of conformity with Scripture or with reason; and the traditions alleged by the Romanists 'we reject...because they are neither in Scripture, nor can otherwise sufficiently be proved by any reason to be of God'. His own definition of tradition safeguarded its importance and affirmed its rightful place. 'Lest therefore the name of tradition should be offensive to any, considering how far by some it hath been and is abused, we mean by traditions, ordinances made in the prime of Christian religion, established with that authority which Christ hath left to his Church for matters indifferent, and in that consideration requisite to be observed, till like authority see just and reasonable cause to alter them.'[1] In such wise, as a contemporary Roman Catholic theologian has testified, 'the theologians of the Church of England achieved a wholesome balance in their principles between the Puritan exclusiveness of Scripture and the excessive concern of some Recusants for a second source of faith'. Their appeal to the first five centuries was to involve difficulties at a later date which were unsuspected by Jewel and Hooker. But 'with this qualification, the Elizabethan Church was by and large true to a patristic and medieval theology which many of their Catholic adversaries had, in spite of the Council of Trent, forsaken'.[2]

The nuances of the Tridentine decree indeed eluded the grasp of some Romanist controversialists of the latter half of the sixteenth century. For example, Melchior Cano's *De Locis Theologicis*, published in 1563, laid down four grounds for the acceptance of tradition. First, that the Church is anterior to the Bible, since it was the guardian of the Gospel before that was committed to writing. Secondly, because not all things pertaining to Christian doctrine were expressed in Scripture; as, for example, the perpetual virginity of the Mother of Christ, the descent of Christ into Hell, the baptism of infants, the conversion of the bread and wine into the Body and Blood of Christ, the procession of the Holy Spirit from the Son and the Trinity in Unity; so that the Church needed to make clear what was only obscurely contained in the Bible. Thirdly, there were many things pertaining to the same Christian doctrine which were not mentioned in Scripture, either plainly or obscurely; as, for example, the words of the Canon of the Mass, the invocation of saints and veneration of images, and the rule that neither Confirmation nor Ordination could be repeated. Fourthly, the Apostles themselves handed down some things in writing and others by word of mouth to their disciples, as was repeatedly testified in the New Testament, particularly in the Epistles; and these oral traditions had been preserved in the Church; and appeal had been made to them by Irenaeus in confuting heretics.[1] Peresius Aaila's *De Divinis, Apostolicis, atque Ecclesiasticis Traditionibus* reverted to a dichotomy of the two sources of faith, Scripture and Tradition, as also did Nicholas Sanders and Thomas Stapleton; so that 'in spite of the Council of Trent, the classical conception all but disappeared from Catholic theology during the Counter-Reformation'.[2]

The contestants on both sides also exhibited a natural tendency to invoke the aid of Church history. In the Praefatio to the *Magdeburg Centuries*, Flacius defended himself against the charge of presumption in undertaking a task which had been discharged already by a series of historians, Eusebius, Socrates, Sozomen, Theodoret, Nicephorus and others, *non aliter quam si post Homerum Iliada auderemus contexere.* He urged that these ancient historians had neglected the development of doctrine, of rites and forms of government in the Church, whereas such subjects should constitute the principal themes of ecclesiastical history. If, however, it should be objected that the treatment of these topics belonged rather to the commentator than to the historian, *qui breviter narrat res*, he replied by pointing to the practice of secular historians of dealing with institutions, laws, decrees and speeches, and claimed the like liberty for the historian of the Church. *Cur non idem liceret in historia ecclesiastica facere, ubi doctrina et alia similia habent eandem rationem?* Accordingly the history of dogma, of the rise and refutation of heresies, of ecclesiastical institutions and forms of worship should be prominent in the modern study of Church history. Furthermore, since in the age of the Reformation such studies could not be divorced from current controversies, particular attention should be given to the growth of corruptions, as well in faith as in practice, in the Church, and the pattern of the primitive Church and the testimony of the Fathers should be set forth as the standard by which to judge declensions in later centuries. Thus Church history should be so written as to form a compendium of knowledge, *in quacunque igitur religionis ecclesiasticarumque rerum parte quis aliquid scire volet, inde haurire poterit*; and at the same time should serve a polemical purpose.[1] Naturally such a method had the properties of a two-edged sword; and Cardinal Baronius' *Annales Ecclesiastici*, a work of more than thirty years' preparation, published in twelve volumes between 1588 and 1607, represented the reply of the Roman Catholics. For, although the *Magdeburg Centuries* were mentioned specifically only a few times throughout these volumes, Baronius was avowedly writing to confute Protestant calumnies. The means of this refutation was to set forth a true and faithful portrait of the Church as it existed in its pristine form, so that its splendour might disperse all shadow and darkness. In executing this task, he resolved to observe the strictest canons of historical accuracy; setting down nothing lightly or inconsiderately, nor which could not be demonstrated by assured testimony, and rejecting learned fables. But the *Annales*, like the *Centuries*, did not conceal its controversial reference; and Baronius intended to show that both the doctrines and institutions of the early Church had been guarded and transmitted to posterity by the unbroken succession of bishops in the see of Rome, to which the primacy, as founded by Christ in the person of St Peter, had demonstrably descended.[2]

During the latter half of the seventeenth century, however, the growth of the historical school of the Benedictines of St Maur introduced new horizons and new methods of patristic study. 'It was an age when for the first time since the Reformation we can discern an international amity of scholarship, which leaps over the walls of religious prejudices as well as the barriers of national antipathy.... With Mabillon, Montfaucon, Ruinart and Tillemont, we seem to have passed beyond all consciousness, even remote consciousness, of the possible theological or controversial effects of their researches.' Bossuet indeed affirmed in his *Exposition of the Doctrine of the Catholic Church in Matters of Controversie*, regarding 'the written and unwritten Word' that 'it is a most certain sign a doctrine comes from the Apostles, when it is embraced by all Christian Churches, without any possibility of shewing its beginning. We cannot choose but receive all that is established after this manner with the submission due to Divine Authority...it being impossible to believe a doctrine, received from the beginning of the Church, can flow from any other source than that of the Apostles.' But the new approach to ecclesiastical history and patristic study produced some unexpected and revolutionary results. Morin's researches into eastern and early western ordination rites had overthrown the statements in the Bull *Exultate Deo* of Pope Eugenius IV in 1439, that the porrection of the instruments and the bestowal of authority to offer sacrifice were the essentials of valid ordination to the priesthood, by demonstrating conclusively that these consisted solely of the imposition of hands with appropriate prayer. Similarly Bossuet's view of the invariability of the doctrines of the Roman Church sustained a severe blow when Du Pin, distinguishing matters of discipline from matters of faith and asserting the former to be variable whilst the latter only were fixed, nevertheless included amongst the mutables prayers, oblations and Masses for the dead, and the invocation and intercession of saints, all of which involved doctrinal tenets. Even worse was Du Pin's complete silence concerning Purgatory, on the ground that he could discover nothing positive in relation to it in the early Fathers, and his contention that they had called the Eucharist the Body and Blood of Christ simply and without elaboration. But if these and other serious omissions characterised Du Pin's *Nouvelle Bibliothèque des Auteurs Ecclésiastiques*, Bossuet was even more disconcerted to discern in his *Histoire des Conciles d'Éphèse et de Chalcédon* a sustained denigration of the Roman primacy, of the dignity of Councils and of the authority of the Fathers. Whereas Du Pin, however, had skirted the circumference of doctrine, the Jesuit Petavius proceeded to lay hands on the ark of the covenant by exposing in *De Theologicis Dogmatibus* the deficiencies in Christology of the ante-Nicene Fathers. In reply to these dangerous tendencies, Emanuel a Schelstrate's *De Disciplina Arcani* found a comprehensive solution for all problems *ex disciplina arcani*. Arguing from the Dominical injunction in Matthew vii. 6, not to give that which is holy to dogs, he deduced that in the early Church the mysteries of the Faith had been expounded only to believers, and that this *disciplina arcani* embraced such dogmas as the Trinity in Unity no less than sacramental rites and ceremonies. Further, since Christ had instituted the Eucharist *in privato coenaculo coram solis Apostolis* and they in turn had celebrated it privately, the doctrine of the Eucharist also had belonged to these secret mysteries of the Church, the *Apology* of Justin Martyr being the exception which proved the rule, since Pliny confessed that he could not penetrate the *arcana* of the Christians. Since this rule had been commanded by Christ and followed by the Fathers, all Protestant criticism could be met by an appeal to its observance. The *disciplina arcani* became thereby an umbrella to cover all things; the silence of the early Fathers concerning the number of the sacraments as seven only, the variations in Eucharistic doctrine before the definition of Transubstantiation, the invocation of saints and the adoration of relics. Thus the reply to Protestants was, not that these and other doctrines and usages were innovations of a later age, but that the *disciplina arcani* of the first seven centuries had concealed both the beliefs and practices of the Church until such time as it became practicable to declare them publicly.[1]

It was evident, however, that this explanation did not adequately cover the facts, and when the Church had recovered from the rationalistic assault of the Encyclopaedists and from the political turmoil of the Revolutionary and Napoleonic era, the way was open and the need urgent for a theory which recognised the fact of development in doctrine whilst retaining continuity with the Bible and the early Church. In the later Middle Ages some canonists had approached the position of a living authority in the Church, vested in the papacy, which replaced both Scripture and its traditional interpretation; and the idea recurred in the course of sixteenth-century controversy. Both Driedo and Pighius adumbrated the notion of doctrinal development, and the latter particularly distinguished a progress from a change of faith, since 'in a progress everything increases within itself, in a change something is transmuted into something else'.[1] Harding also interpreted the continuity of the Church as parallel to the growth of an individual. 'The Church that now is and the Church that was in old time is one Church, as a man in his old age is the same man he was in his youth.'[2] During the nineteenth century the concept of evolution seemed to possess the key to unlock many problems in theology as well as in other disciplines. Dr Owen Chadwick has traced the endeavour of Newman's *Essay on the Development of Christian Doctrine* to create 'a revised idea of tradition, which corresponds within the Roman Church to those other revisions of the idea of tradition, which the new critical history was forcing upon Christian thinkers'.[3] But the decree of the Council of Trent, by excluding ecclesiastical traditions, had required as a foundation for dogmas 'unwritten traditions which were received by the Apostles from the lips of Christ himself, or by the same Apostles at the dictation of the Holy Spirit, and were handed down and have come down to us'; and which also had been 'preserved by unbroken succession in the Church'. This definition imposed upon apologists the task of demonstrating by historical evidence both the apostolic provenance and the unbroken transmission of any doctrine called in question. The duty could hardly be discharged, granted the validity of the new methods of historical criticism. Accordingly the argument adumbrated by Schelstrate was applied by Professor Perrone to establish a twofold character of tradition, as latent and patent; so that the former kind might become the source of a dogmatic definition, although its presence in the Church had been undetected for several centuries. The application of this new interpretation of *disciplina arcani* was seen in the promulgation of the dogma of the Immaculate Conception of the Virgin Mary in 1854. The biblical passages brought forward included the *Protoevangelium* of Genesis iii. 15 ('it shall bruise thy head and thou shalt bruise his heel'), which the Vulgate rendered *ipsa conteret caput tuum*, and the Angelic salutation in Luke i. 28 ('Hail, thou that art highly favoured'), where the Vulgate translated κεχαριτωμένη by *gratia plena*. This slender biblical testimony was reinforced by the argument from tradition, since Irenaeus, Justin Martyr and Tertullian had used the Eve–Mary antithesis to show that, whereas the former brought death and sin into the world, the latter bore the Word who brought salvation and immortality to light. Thus the prolonged controversy between

Dominicans who opposed, and Franciscans who supported the belief and were now strengthened by the advocacy of the Jesuits, was brought to an end.

Almost a century later, the definition as an article of faith of the Bodily Assumption of the Virgin Mary provided a stronger example of the reliance upon latent tradition. Admittedly, it had been unknown during the first four centuries of the Church; and the difficulties of providing evidence for its alleged historical character were considerable. The definition *Munificentissimus Deus* accordingly began by emphasising the intimate connexion between the dogma of the Immaculate Conception and that of the Assumption (*arctissime enim haec duo privilegia inter se connectuntur*) and recited the contemporary *consensus fidelium*, as represented by petitions to the pope in behalf of the promulgation and by the testimony of the bishops, almost all of whom (*unanima fere voce*) approved. After references to liturgical evidence both from west and east, the earliest Fathers cited in support of the doctrine were John of Damascus and Germanus of Constantinople in the late seventh and early eighth centuries, followed by a catena of scholastic theologians and their successors, including Bishop Amadeus of Lausanne, St Anthony of Padua, Albertus Magnus, St Thomas Aquinas, St Bonaventura, St Bernardino of Siena, Bellarmine, St François de Sales, St Alfonso di Liguori, Peter Canisius and Suarez. The scriptural citations were both elusive and recondite in character. From Psalm cxxxii. 8 ('Arise O Lord into thy resting place, thou, and the ark of thy strength'), a parallel was drawn between the *Arca sanctificationis tuae* and the Ark of the Covenant on the one hand, made of indestructible wood and placed within the temple, and on the other hand the Blessed Virgin Mary, whose body was likewise preserved from corruption and exalted in glory to heaven. Similarly Psalm xlv, verses 10 and 14–16, with its reference to the king's daughter 'led unto the king in broidered work' *in templum regis*, was interpreted of Mary, the queen entering in triumph into the king's hall in heaven and sitting by the side of the Divine Redeemer (*Reginam in regiam Caelorum aulam per triumphum ingredientem ac Divini Redemptoris assidentem lateri*). Again, the Song of Songs, chapter iii, verse 6, 'Who is this that cometh up out of the wilderness like pillars of smoke, perfumed with myrrh and frankincense, with all powders of the merchant?', was understood of Mary, *quae una cum Divino Sponso ad Caelorum aulam evehitur*; and was further supported by chapter iv, verse 8, beginning 'Come with me from Lebanon, my bride' and continuing in the Vulgate, *coronaberis de capite Amana, de vertice Sanir et Hermon*, and by chapter vi, verse 10, 'Who is she that looketh forth as the morning, fair as the moon, clear as the sun, terrible as an army with banners?' (*Quae est ista, quae progreditur quasi aurora consurgens pulchra ut luna, electa ut sol, terribilis ut castrorum acies ordinata?*). St Bonaventura also had applied to Mary verse 5 of chapter viii, 'Who is this that cometh up from the wilderness, leaning upon her beloved?' (*Quae est ista, quae ascendit de deserto, deliciis affluens, innixa super dilectum suum?*); and St Anthony of Padua had adduced Isaiah lx. 13, 'And I will make the place of my feet glorious' (*Et locum pedum meorum glorificabo*), in support of the belief. From the New Testament only two direct citations were proffered, the angelic salutation, *Ave, gratia plena: Dominus tecum, Benedicta tu in mulieribus* (Luke i. 28): and the twelfth chapter of Revelation, verses 1–6, particularly the sign of 'a woman arrayed with the sun' (*Muliere amicta sole*), in which the Scholastic doctors saw prefigured the Assumption (*Assumptionem Deiparae Virginis significatam viderunt*). Although therefore the definition professed to accept Scripture *tamquam ultimo fundamento*, its dependence upon the Bible was that of hypothetical deductions, such as that 'it seems almost impossible to conclude that She, who conceived, bore, nourished with her own milk, held in her arms and clasped to her bosom, Christ, would be separated from Him in body (even though not in spirit) after this earthly life' (*Quamobrem quasi impossibile videtur eam cernere, quae Christum concepit, peperit, suo lacte aluit, eumque inter ulnas habuit, pectorique obstrinxit suo, ab eodem post terrestrem hanc vitam, etsi non anima, corpore tamen separatam*).

'There is an historic Christianity as well as a dogmatic, and the dogmatic can never be rightly understood except in the light of the historic.' The judgement of R. C. Trench has an evident relevance to the question of the relationship of Scripture to oral tradition and also of theology to history, particularly in respect of the definition of the Assumption of the Virgin Mary. The contrast between the silence of Scripture and early tradition on the one hand and the promulgation of the dogma *de fide* on the other hand would seem to have gone far towards realising the fear expressed by Fr Tavard in regard to the fourteenth-century dichotomy of Scripture and Tradition; namely, that 'it threw open a door, by way of a supposed superiority of the Church over Holy Writ, to the idea that the Church had her own revelation, independent of that which the Apostles recorded in their writings'.[1] The dogmatic element in Christianity must necessarily have a sufficient foundation in Scripture, and theological doctrines purporting to rest upon events of history must have an adequate basis of historical evidence. It would be difficult to perceive that either condition was satisfied in *Munificentissimus Deus*. Nor would the task be easy of reconciling the definition with the requirements of the decree of the Council of Trent, so far as concerned apostolic origins and unbroken transmission. During the latter half of the nineteenth century and the first half of its successor, indeed, there has been a marked growth in appreciation of the value and authority of ecclesiastical tradition and a more sympathetic understanding of its place in the formulation of Christian truth. Partly this represented a reaction against its depreciation and neglect in the 'age of enlightenment', and in part a recognition that tradition offered a bulwark against the destructive assault of biblical criticism. Moreover it has proved congenial to the contemporary oecumenical endeavour towards ecclesiastical *rapprochement*. But the cumulative effect of these tendencies has emphasised the necessity for dogmatic definitions *de fide* to be soundly and surely supported by a sufficiency of scriptural testimony and by an authentic tradition of history. Chillingworth, indeed, notwithstanding his stout assertion of *sola Scriptura*, allowed in respect of its defenders that 'whatsoever else they believe besides it and the plain irrefragable consequences of it, well may they hold as a matter of opinion', though 'neither can they with coherence to their own grounds believe it themselves nor require the belief of it of others'. The distinction between beliefs held by individuals as pious opinions and doctrines formally defined by the Church as necessary to be believed for eternal salvation is too well known and generally accepted to need emphasis or elaboration. In regard to dogmas *de fide* which lack both clear apostolic provenance and evidence of unbroken transmission in the Church, the student of Church history can but say with St Augustine: *Quum Dominus tacuerit, quis nostrum dicat, Illa vel Illa sunt?: aut si dicere audeat, unde probat?*

CHAPTER IV

CHURCH, STATE AND EDUCATION SINCE 1815

'*Libera chiesa in libero stato.* Such is the aphorism in which the maker of Italian unity summed up the ideal of statesmanship for the solution of the perennial problem of the two powers. Whether or no this ideal can be attained is doubtful; that it never has been attained is certain.' When Dr Figgis accepted Cavour's maxim and lamented its impracticability in 1911, on the one hand the formal disproof of his pessimism by the enactment of the Church of Scotland Act of 1921 lay still in the future; but so also did the advent of the totalitarian State on the other hand with its unequivocal negation of the principle of ecclesiastical freedom. With the break-up of the medieval unity of the western Church at the Reformation, it was natural that the relationship of Church and State in the territories which threw off the papal supremacy should assume new and controversial forms; and equally inevitable that the balance should incline to the side of the temporal power and to the disadvantage of the ecclesiastical. When traditional prelates like Stephen Gardiner appealed to the testimony of the Bible in favour of the godly prince and against the authority of the papacy, it was evident that a change had come over the ecclesiastical climate. Whether in the form of a royal supremacy as in Sweden and England, or in that of civic councils as in the Swiss cities of Zürich and Geneva, or of the territorial princes of Germany, the temporal power was asserting its authority against the spiritual. But always it was axiomatic that the prince should be a godly prince, that is, a Christian ruler, concerned for the propagation and defence of the true faith. When James VI of Scotland, on his succession to the English throne and to the Supreme Governorship of the Church of England, described his office as that of 'Professor, Maintainer and Defender of the True, Christian, Catholic and Apostolic Faith according to the Teaching of the Primitive Church', he expressed, somewhat fulsomely and flamboyantly perhaps, the principle underlying the function of the godly prince in relation to religion. Nor was the phenomenon confined to Protestant princes. The long struggle of Louis XIV in behalf of the *Regale* and the Declaration of Gallican Liberties, and the ecclesiastical reforms of Joseph II of Austria testified to the resolve of Catholic sovereigns to be masters in their own house; and the latter's flirtation with Febronianism showed that he was not averse to embarrassing the papacy by supporting a revival of Conciliarism. But these were wounds inflicted on Rome in the house of its friends and *soi-disant* defenders. Another face of things was seen when the French Revolution led to an extreme conflict with the

Church, resulting in overt disavowal of Christianity and the substitution of the cult of the goddess of reason.

Professor Latreille indeed, breaking with the interpretation of the religious policy of the Constituent Assembly set forth by Aulard and Mathiez, has seen in the Civil Constitution of the Clergy the precursor of the modern totalitarian State. 'De là cette idée de recourir au serment — acte religieux — pour lier les magistrats et les citoyens à la chose publique; de là l'obéissance totale, comparable à une obéissance religieuse, exigée pour l'État, pour la Loi, et en cas d'insoumission, ce fanatisme à faire triompher les principes nécessaires à l'ordre social; de là cette manie, qui nous étonne, de légiférer sur les choses ecclésiastiques.'[1] In accordance with this interpretation, the Civil Constitution, and particularly the requirement of the civil registration of births, marriages and deaths, marked the inauguration of the modern, secular State and the rupture of the traditional alliance of Church and State in Europe. 'Il n'est pas douteux que, rompant définitivement avec la tradition qui laissait ce service public au clergé national, mettant fin en somme à la fusion du spirituel et du temporel qui subsistait depuis le Moyen Âge, elle n'ait, le 20 septembre 1792, fixé le régime moderne de l'état civil et amorcé la séparation de l'État et de l'Église.'[2] Although the Revolution was submerged in the Napoleonic Empire and later overthrown by the victorious allies, the new Europe of the nineteenth century was no longer, save in outward appearance, that of absolute monarchs and benevolent despots; for the principles of 1789 had taken root in a number of perhaps surprising quarters and were to produce a crop of difficult problems in the relations of Church and State, particularly in respect of their competing claims in the field of education.

It was natural that education should become a field of conflict, because it had enjoyed a prominent place in the plans and ideals of the principal reformers in the sixteenth century. Both Luther and Melanchthon were inspired by zeal for education. The former issued in 1524 an 'Appeal to the Municipalities of Germany', in which he advocated the provision of schools and of teaching in Latin, Greek, Hebrew and other liberal arts as an essential *praeparatio evangelica.* Ranke indeed held this manifesto to be as significant in its particular sphere as the 'Address to the Christian Nobility' in its field. Luther took steps to revive the Wittenberg school, and within a year of the publication of his *Appeal* the cities of Magdeburg, Nordhausen, Halberstadt, Gotha, Eisleben and Nuremberg had responded to his call. His *Church Order* of 1528 placed the establishment of good schools for children amongst the three indispensable necessities; whilst in his preface to Justus Menius' *Christian Economy* and in his own sermon *On the Duty of Keeping Children at School* in 1530, he reverted to the themes of the necessity of classical learning for the ministry and of a sound general education of youth for the service of the State. In

Melanchthon's inaugural address as professor of Greek at Wittenberg, he discoursed of *The Improvement of the Studies of Youth*; and Lutheran states maintained theological faculties in their universities for the education of the ministry. As might be expected, Zwingli was no less insistent on the need of sound education both for the clergy and laity of Zürich. In the Great Minster the clergy were to read and expound the Bible publicly for an hour each day in Hebrew, Greek and Latin; and provision was also made for public lectures on the Scriptures. With the dissolution of monastic corporations in 1524, education in Zürich enjoyed first claim on the available revenues, the funds of the Great Minster being devoted in part to the endowment of a gymnasium, whilst Zwingli himself became rector of the *Carolinum*, as the united scholastic foundations were called. Only his early death on the field of Kappel prevented Zürich from enjoying the full fruition of his educational schemes. Even more famous and far-reaching in their influence were the educational reforms of Calvin at Geneva, where a graduated scheme of instruction from the primary stage to preparation for the ministry was established, culminating in the renowned College of the city. The curriculum embraced Latin, Greek, logic, rhetoric and exercises in style and declamation; whilst religious instruction consisted of the Lord's Prayer, psalm-singing and exposition of the Ten Commandments and the Apostles' Creed. It was a pardonable exaggeration which ascribed to Calvin's scheme of education the alleged ability of the youth of Geneva to give a reason for their faith 'like a doctor of the Sorbonne'. Compared with such provision, education in England reaped not a harvest but mere gleanings from the Reformation. The promise of Colet's foundation of St Paul's School, where teaching was to combine the best Greek and Latin classical authors with religious instruction according to his catechism, together with Cranmer's project for the application of cathedral revenues to theological education, were alike unfulfilled. The dissolution of the monastic corporations furnished spoils for the royal coffers and for avaricious courtiers rather than means for the further endowment and establishment of grammar schools; and the generality of such schools bearing the names of Henry VIII and Edward VI are memorials of missed opportunity rather than the realisation of the ideals of reformers.

On the other hand the Counter-Reformation, particularly in the hands of its most militant and influential agent, the Society of Jesus, placed education in the forefront of its campaign for the defeat of Protestantism. The papal Bull *Regimini militantis* of 1540, constituting the Jesuit Order, laid especial stress *nominatim per puerorum ac rudium in Christianismo institutionem*; and the vow taken by Ignatius Loyola at Mass on his election as first General in 1541 included the promise: 'And I further vow that I will teach boys in the principles of the faith according to the Bull and the Constitution'; which he proceeded forthwith to fulfil. Likewise the vows of the professed and formal coadjutors of the Society emphasised the duty of instructing children in the faith; and the Constitutions of the Society of 1558 provided for the education of its members and for the opening of 'public schools, where it may conveniently be done, at least for humane studies (*in disciplinis humanioribus*)', and in which youths were educated for secular professions as well as for the priesthood. From this process of educational experiment and experience was developed the *Ratio atque Institutio Studiorum Societatis Jesu*, which crystallised the Jesuit system. As basis and foundation of education were the humanities, Greek and Latin languages and literature being the principal subjects of instruction, and also the preliminaries to philosophy, and next came theology, in which the *Ratio Studiorum* had its culmination as the intellectual equipment for the clergy, whilst careful provision was made that the *externi* 'may be well instructed in all that relates to Christian learning'. Thus from the elementary teaching of children by catechism, through the education of youth for secular professions, to the training of the priesthood, the Jesuit Order furnished potent and effectual means for the combating of Protestantism. It was indeed their success in the field of education, amounting in some countries to a virtual monopoly, which provoked jealousy and opposition from the temporal rulers. The dissolution of the Order in 1773 by Clement XIV under pressure from Roman Catholic sovereigns marked the beginning of their decline; and the 'principles of 1789' augured ill for their future in the realm of education. With the coming of the nineteenth century 'the school-question represented perhaps the most sensitive point of the relations between church and state. The rise of the modern secularist state, among whose functions universal education is of primary importance, precipitated a quarrel with the church, which still awaits a satisfactory solution.'[1] Accordingly much of the problem of the relationship of Church and State since 1815 has centred in the field of education.

In the home of revolution itself, the Napoleonic University, which Lamennais stigmatised as an agent 'to give over the greater part of the nation to a brutalising savagery while allowing a small minority to rise to a kind of instructed barbarism', had maintained widespread control of national education in France. Secondary and higher education was almost its exclusive preserve, whilst in the comparatively neglected field of primary education the Church enjoyed a dominant influence as a consequence of an ordinance of 1824 and through the part played by the local clergy in primary schools. The only sphere of higher education in which the Church enjoyed freedom from State control was that of the diocesan *petits séminaires*, which being designed for the recruitment of the clergy, were by an ordinance of 1814 exempted from the authority of the University. During the regime of the restored Bourbons the administration turned a blind eye to the extension of these seminaries by the provision, either within their own premises or by the opening of *écoles ecclésiastiques*, of educational facilities for sons of the bourgeoisie and nobility. Moreover in eight cases the bishop of the diocese had entrusted the direction of these schools to members of the Society of Jesus, reconstituted by Pius VII in 1814, whose association with them increased the suspicion entertained in anti-clerical quarters. As a result of hostile criticism, a commission was appointed in 1828 to report on national education, and to assist its investigations a questionnaire was addressed to the episcopate, directed to ascertaining in particular the proportion of pupils in the Church schools wearing the soutane and whether the masters were laymen or priests, and if the latter, whether secular or religious.

Between the appointment of the commission and its report, however, the administration issued an ordinance in April transferring the control of primary schools from the bishops to that of local committees composed of nine members, only one-third of whom were nominated by the bishop. When the report was published in the following month, its principal provisions restricted the ecclesiastical schools to the training of boys destined for the priesthood, and only by a narrow majority of five votes to four allowed Jesuits to teach in these *petits séminaires*. In June the administration issued further ordinances, requiring the eight ecclesiastical secondary schools under the direction of the Jesuits to be brought within the control of the University, and their teachers to affirm in writing that they did not belong to a religious order not legally established in France. Various detailed regulations also prescribed the quota of pupils to be admitted to the Church schools, and their number and location.

Accordingly Lamennais resolved to accept the challenge and published in 1829 *Des Progrès de la révolution et de la guerre contre l'Église*, in which he raised the standard of revolt by demanding freedom for the Church from the shackles of the State and its alliance with the forces of liberalism. With the overthrow by the July revolution of 1830 of the Bourbon monarchy, and the substitution of the bourgeois rule of Louis Philippe, Lamennais took the further step of founding a daily newspaper *L'Avenir* to propagate his ideas, affirming the four fundamental freedoms of complete religious liberty, liberty of education, freedom of the press and liberty of association. With the establishment of the triumvirate of Montalembert, Lacordaire and Lamennais and the foundation of the *Agence générale pour la défense de la liberté religieuse*, the campaign gained increasing momentum, and the education question was forced rapidly to the foreground. Petitions were organised from various parts of the country, to the number of 379, demanding the abolition of the monopoly of the University and freedom for the Church to control its own schools. Even more significant was the resort to 'Catholic action' by the establishment in Paris itself in May 1831 of an *école libre*, without seeking the prior official authorisation required by law. When the administration, unable to ignore the challenge thus explicitly offered, resolved upon prosecution, Montalembert, having become a member of the upper house of parliament in June, claimed the right of trial by his peers, and the case resulted in the infliction of a fine of 100 francs. The penalty was *pour rire* in its evident disproportion to the *cause célèbre*; and what had been begun in the capital was continued in provincial centres. Thus education had been brought into the front of the contest between Church and State in France, where it was to remain throughout the political and constitutional vicissitudes of the following century.

When the thunderbolts of papal displeasure descended upon the head of Lamennais, after a short interval of submission he broke with his past, leaving his colleagues to continue the struggle for educational freedom. It was a cause entirely congenial to Montalembert, who published in December 1843 a pamphlet, *Du devoir des catholiques dans la question de la liberté d'enseignement*, described as *un long cri de guerre*; in which he showed that Lamennais' mantle fitted admirably to his shoulders, by demanding the abolition of the University monopoly, and by exhorting his fellow-churchmen to embark upon a public crusade for freedom of education, for the success of which *il ne leur manque qu'une seule chose, c'est le courage*. Political campaigning, however, like adversity, makes strange bedfellows; and Montalembert found himself somewhat unequally yoked with the fervent Ultramontane, Louis Veuillot, editor of *L'Univers*, and with Mgr Parisis, bishop of Langres, who had learned from Mgr Van Bommel, bishop of Liège, the value of publicity in such matters, and published in December 1843 his pamphlet on *Liberté de l'enseignement.* A reply to these manifestos from the administration came in February 1844 in the shape of an Education Bill, whose provisions restricted the number of pupils to be admitted to *petits séminaires* and required all teachers to take an oath that they were not members of any unauthorised religious order. The issue was brought thus into the political arena, and the episcopate united its forces in opposition; whilst Montalembert attacked the Bill in the upper house, where amendments favourable to the Church were inserted. When the measure reached the lower house, therefore, Guizot withdrew it in order to frustrate the tactics of his adroit opponent, Thiers, who hoped to bring down the government by demanding even more stringent tests for teachers. The withdrawal, however, was evidently only temporary; and Montalembert, in anticipation of the renewal of the struggle, organised a *Comité pour la défense de la liberté religieuse*, with local committees in the several departments, and enrolled members under the maxim *Dieu et Mon Droit*. With the battle-formations thus mustering between the 'sons of the Crusaders' and the 'sons of Voltaire', the *Comité* perfected its organisation with an eye to the forthcoming parliamentary elections in 1846, with the result that the *parti catholique* secured the return of 140 deputies pledged to support its programme.

In 1847, therefore, the administration introduced another Education Bill, which, whilst abolishing the requirement of the *brevet de capacité* and the certificate of morality in respect of teachers and diminishing the control of the University, retained the conditions of a university degree and the oath required of teachers that they did not belong to an unauthorised congregation. These restrictions were unacceptable to Montalembert and his allies, and the controversy had not reached a settlement when the Revolution of 1848 transformed the political situation. Not until Louis Napoleon had secured the Presidency was the matter settled by the Loi Falloux of 1850. By its provisions the monopoly of the University was abolished; and in place of the former *Conseil Royal de l'Université* there was set up a *Conseil Supérieur de l'Instruction Publique*, consisting of twenty-seven members, of whom the University contributed only eight, whilst the interests of religion were represented by four bishops, two Protestant pastors and one rabbi. In the sphere of local government, the existing twenty *Académies* were replaced by eighty-six *Conseils Académiques*, corresponding to the administrative departments, in which the University influence was even slighter. Side by side with the State-controlled schools the existence of *écoles libres* was formally recognised, in which there was no ban on the service as teachers of members of religious congregations, whilst the authority of State inspectors in voluntary schools was confined to points of morality, hygiene and health. In primary schools, moral and religious instruction was to be given, and the *petits séminaires* were maintained in their privileges and without limitation of numbers. Although the measure represented so substantial a victory for Montalembert, it encountered the violent denunciation of *L'Univers* and the bishop of Langres; but the rapid multiplication of religious orders during the next decade increased ecclesiastical influence in both primary and secondary schools. With the increasing political difficulties between Napoleon III and Pius IX, and the consequential cooling of relations between the emperor and the episcopate, however, the administration began to encroach piecemeal on the favourable provisions of the Loi Falloux, particularly under the direction of MM. Rouland and Duruy, by increasing the influence of the State schools at the expense of those under ecclesiastical control. As the Second Empire approached its end, an uneasy equilibrium between Church and State in the field of education was maintained, not without difficulty.

Even more fluctuating was their relationship during the tortuous and tempestuous history of the Third Republic. At first, the Assembly in 1875 allowed the erection of university colleges, or *facultés libres*, by the Church or by other associations, with the right to confer degrees, subject only to the requirement that candidates for graduation in the non-State universities should be examined by *jurys mixtes*, composed of an equal number of professors in the State universities and in the *universités libres*, and chosen by the Minister of Education. By virtue of this law a Catholic University was forthwith established in Paris. The Indian summer, however, was short-lived; for in 1876 a Bill to deprive the Catholic universities of their right to confer degrees was defeated by only a small margin in the Senate, after passing the Chamber by a large majority, and in the following year Gambetta raised his war-cry of *Le cléricalisme, voilà l'ennemi*. The application of this maxim to education was summarised in the formula *l'obligation, la gratuité, la laïcité*; namely, that the national educational system should be compulsory, free and non-clerical. In 1879 the Loi Falloux was altered materially, in a direction unfavourable to the Church, by the exclusion of bishops and clergy from the *Conseil Supérieur de l'Instruction Publique* and from the local *Conseils Académiques* respectively; whilst the right of conferring degrees was restricted to the State universities, and other institutions for higher education were forbidden to assume the title of 'university'. At the same time the attack was launched against unauthorised religious congregations, itself a subsidiary skirmish in the campaign for the extinction of clerical control of education. In 1882 a law was carried abolishing religious instruction in public primary schools (though allowing it outside the school buildings), and excluding the clergy from the direction of these schools. Five years later a further measure required the replacement of members of Catholic teaching orders still employed in State schools by lay instructors; and the severity of the blow was only mitigated by the gallant reply of the Church in the foundation of *écoles libres*, in which by the end of a decade nearly a million and a half children were receiving education. The general shape of things to come was becoming evident however, and with the premiership of M. Combes in 1902 events moved to the expected climax with a frontal assault on the religious congregations, both authorised and unauthorised, because of their educational work. By the end of the year some 12,000 Church schools were under sentence of extinction. Next came the fate of secondary schools, since the Catholic schools in 1900 had 91,000 male pupils against 81,000 in State secondary schools. In 1904 a law was carried to suppress during the course of a decade all education by religious congregations; and in the following year the *coup de grâce* was given to the traditional association of Church and State in France by the *Loi de Séparation*.

The prominence given to the schools question in the relations of Church and State during the nineteenth century was evidence alike of the importance of the control of education of youth, and of the emergence of a new policy in several European countries in respect both of the Church and of education. Item 45 of the *Syllabus Errorum* of Pius IX in 1864 denounced the erroneous conclusion that 'the whole administration of public schools in which the youth of any Christian state is educated (with the sole exception for sufficient reason of episcopal seminaries), can and should be so arranged that no right should be recognised to any other authority of intervention in the administration of the schools, the ordering of studies, the conferment of degrees or the choice and approval of teachers'. Similarly Item 47 censured the opinion that 'the best interest of civil society requires that public schools, which are open to all children from every class of the people, and public Institutes, designed for the teaching of literary and more advanced disciplines and for the education of youth, should be withdrawn from all control, directive power and supervision of the Church, and should be subjected to the entire direction of the civil and political authority and thereby to the pleasure of these rulers and to the standard of the common opinions of the age'. Furthermore chapter xv of the schema *De Ecclesia*, laid before the Vatican Council on 21 January 1870, specified 'certain particular rights of the Church in relation to Civil Society', and placed first amongst 'violations of the rights of the Church on the part of civil governments', the 'laicising of education, so that all consideration of religion is excluded, and the Church prohibited from all control and from providing instruction in the Catholic religion'.

When therefore Bismarck sought grounds for a challenge to the Roman Church, he found a ready pretext to hand in the definition of the papal magisterium and infallibility by the Vatican Council. The recent publication of documents between July 1870 and December 1872, from the Prussian Ministry of the Interior in *Die Vorgeschichte des Kulturkampfes* has confirmed the previous impression that the campaign was the subject of careful preparation, together with evidence that the Prussian civil service was persuaded that it was essentially a defensive action against the aggressive policy of Rome. It was not without significance, therefore, that the first shot to be fired took the form of an educational law of March 1872, passed by the Prussian *Landtag* at the instance of Dr Falk, which transferred the right of inspection of primary schools from ecclesiastics to officials of the State; and that this was followed by an administrative order in June excluding religious orders from participation in public education. With the famous May Laws of 1873, which extended the intervention of the State into properly ecclesiastical matters, the conflict became an open assertion of the determination of the modern totalitarian State to control all aspects of the lives of its citizens. But if Bismarck had pushed issues to an extreme, the principles of his policy found echoes in other countries. In Austria the papacy received the most unexpected, if not the worst, wounds in the house of its friends; for the definition of papal infallibility was made the ground for a denunciation of the concordat of 1855 between the emperor and the pope; and this was followed by a series of measures affecting both primary and higher education. In 1869 the certificates of proficiency issued by the diocesan seminaries were subjected to governmental control, the oversight of Catholic schools was entrusted to inspectors nominated by the provincial governors, instead of as heretofore to the bishops, so that the episcopate was left only with the supervision of religious instruction, and even in this sphere new and restrictive regulations were published. In 1873 the universities likewise were brought under State control, the episcopate being excluded from the part which it had hitherto enjoyed in their administration, and Protestant faculties of theology being given the same position as Catholic. Josephism was evidently far from extinct in Austria.

Under very different circumstances education became a controversial issue likewise in England, where the conflict however lay not between the State and the Church, but rather between the several churches. Until 1833, primary education had been the province of voluntary service and had been undertaken almost exclusively by the several churches, functioning chiefly through the 'National Society for promoting the education of the poor in the principles of the established church' and the 'British and Foreign Schools Society' which provided biblical instruction whilst eschewing denominational teaching. These two societies shared in proportion to the number of schools under their control the first parliamentary grant of £20,000 in 1833 'for the purposes of education'. Traditionally the Nonconformists had been staunch supporters of the principle of voluntaryism in education, believing that it was no business of the State to educate children, but that this responsibility lay upon the parents, helped by the churches and philanthropic societies. In 1843 indeed Edward Baines declared that 'it is not the province of a government to educate the people, and the admission of the principle that it is its province could lead to practical consequences fatal to civil and religious liberty'. Furthermore, since religious instruction must be integral to education, this even more emphatically must be the province of the churches. The established church, on the other hand, welcomed the support of the State for its primary schools and desired the religious teaching given in them to be based upon its own catechism.

With the increase of the parliamentary grant to £30,000 in 1839, and the appointment of a special committee of the privy council to deal with education and its project in the same year for State inspection of the schools, the divergence of view between the Church of England and the Nonconformists became steadily clearer. When Sir James Graham's Factory Bill of 1843 proposed that compulsory education for factory children should be provided under the direction of the established church, it provoked determined opposition from Nonconformity. For, although the religious instruction was not to be formally denominational but restricted to exposition of the Scriptures, the factory schools were to be under the management of the parish clergyman, churchwardens and four persons chosen by the Justices of the Peace in Petty Sessions, a committee whose personnel inclined definitely towards the established church. Thanks to the vigorous organisation of protests from the Nonconformist churches, the offending clauses were withdrawn. During the next quarter of a century, however, the scope of the problem was widened without any solution to the ecclesiastical difficulty being found. The amount of the State subvention increased steadily and substantially, the committee of the privy council gave place to an official department of education and the demand for a national system of education increased both in volume and in force. Meantime also the attitude of the Nonconformist churches was undergoing a change, at least of emphasis, as the testimony of R. W. Dale made clear. For by 1861 Dale had come to make 'a clear distinction between the voluntary principle in religion and the voluntary principle in education', and was convinced that 'the one did not necessarily involve the other'. During the next quinquennium his mind advanced rapidly and firmly to the conclusion that the State must provide a national, compulsory and free system of education. 'My position is this,' he avowed in 1867, 'the child has a right to receive elementary education; the State can enforce that right, and ought to enforce it; if the parents are able to pay for that education, they ought to be made to pay; if they are too poor, the right of the child must still be acknowledged, and the State must provide education from public funds.'[1]

The next issue to be faced therefore was whether the Nonconformists preferred a national system of purely secular education, or whether they were prepared to compromise on some programme of religious instruction within the national system. In the latter case the controversy would be with the established church, because of its possession of the great majority of primary schools; and the acute question would arise concerning the character of the religious instruction to be given, since Anglicans would press for the use of the Prayer Book Catechism and Nonconformists for biblical teaching only. When Forster's Education Bill was enacted in 1870, it strove to reconcile the opposing points of view; for it neither abolished nor confiscated the existing denominational schools but incorporated them into a national system of education, virtually doubling the previous grants to them (on condition that they reached satisfactory educational and hygienic standards). On the other hand it provided for the building of board schools to supply the deficiencies of voluntary schools, in areas where they did not exist or were inadequate for the population. At the committee stage a solution of the religious problem was sought by the insertion of the famous Cowper–Temple clause, by which religious instruction in board schools was to exclude any 'catechism or religious formulary distinctive of any particular denomination', but to consist of exposition of the Bible. As a compromise, the Act did not satisfy the Nonconformists. Dale indeed declared that 'not even at the bidding of a Liberal Ministry will we consent to any proposition which, under cover of an educational measure, empowers one religious denomination to levy a rate for teaching its creed and maintaining its worship. On this point compromise is impossible; our minds are made up, our decision is irrevocable. We respect Mr Forster; we honour Mr Gladstone; but we are determined that England shall not again be cursed with the bitterness and strife, from which we hoped we had escaped for ever by the abolition of the church rate.'[1] Nor was the ensuing and embittered controversy to be stilled until the Butler Education Act of 1944, since several efforts to achieve a solution during the interval were wrecked on the rocks of ecclesiastical conflict. More than two generations after the Forster Act of 1870 moreover, Mr Bernard Manning's posthumous history of *The Protestant Dissenting Deputies* echoed ancient war-cries, by its references to 'the malignant shadow of Sir James Graham' falling across education, and to 'the woodenness of Gladstone and the maliciousness of Forster', and by its melancholy conclusion that 'the seeds of clerical and anti-clerical struggles, hitherto unknown in England, were sown by the ex-Quaker Forster and watered by Whitehall agnostics'.[2]

The conflicts of the nineteenth century, however, were but the prelude to far more acute and menacing problems, raised by the rise of the totalitarian regimes of the present century with their resolute determination not merely to wrest the control of education from the churches, but also to substitute for Christian instruction the inculcation of their own particular secularist ideology. Article 121 of the Constitution of the U.S.S.R. of 1936 indeed states simply that 'citizens of the U.S.S.R. have the right to education. This right is ensured by universal compulsory elementary education, by education free of charge including higher education'; whilst Article 124 declares that 'in order to ensure to citizens freedom of conscience, the church in the U.S.S.R. shall be separated from the state and the school from the church. Freedom of religious worship and freedom of anti-religious propaganda shall be recognised for all citizens.'[1] Even if the terms of the latter Article had been inviolably kept and no persecution of the Church had been undertaken, the exclusion of religion from the State system of education and the restriction of the liberty of the Church to public worship without the means of education and propaganda, would have seriously jeopardised its position. At the other extreme, Mussolini's *La Dottrina del Fascismo* affirmed that 'Fascism is a religious conception in which man is seen in his immanent relationship with a superior law and with an objective Will that transcends the particular individual and raises him to conscious membership of a spiritual society'. Accordingly, 'for the Fascist, everything is in the State, and nothing human or spiritual exists, much less has value, outside the State'; and therefore 'the Fascist State, the highest and most powerful form of personality, is a force, but a spiritual force, which takes over all the forms of the moral and intellectual life of man'. Indeed, 'Fascism, in short, is not only the giver of laws and the founder of institutions, but the educator and promoter of spiritual life'. From this it followed that 'for Fascism the State is an absolute before which individuals and groups are relative'; and therefore that 'the Fascist State does not remain indifferent to the fact of religion in general and to that particular positive religion which is Italian Catholicism. The State has no theology, but it has an ethic. In the Fascist State religion is looked upon as one of the deepest manifestations of the spirit; it is therefore not only respected but defended and protected.'[1]

In the case of the Nazi party, the Twenty-five Points of February 1920 embraced in Item 20 the demand that 'the State must undertake a thorough reconstruction of our national system of education', so that 'with the first dawn of intelligence, the schools must aim at teaching the pupil to know what the State stands for'; whilst Item 23 promised 'liberty for all religious denominations in the State, in so far as they are not a danger to it and do not militate against the moral sense of the German race'. This article continued to affirm that 'the Party, as such, stands for a positive Christianity, but does not bind itself in the matter of creed to any particular confession'. The semi-official interpretation of 'positive Christianity' given by Rosenberg, however, was that it was 'opposed to the negative Christianity of the dominations of priests and witches, both going back to Etrusco-Asiatic conceptions.... Negative Christianity (Roman Catholicism, and, in a lesser degree, Protestantism) emphasizes its Syriac-Etruscan tradition, abstract dogmas and old sacred customs, positive Christianity recalls to life the forces of the nordic blood.' In face of this definition, it was of merely theoretical relevance that the Political and Economic Programme of the Party, in 1927, should profess acceptance of 'complete liberty of creed and conscience' and 'special protection for the Christian denominations', since this was followed by the aim of 'suppression and discouragement of dogmas which are opposed to the German moral sense and are injurious to the State and nation'.[1] Positive Christianity thus diluted by doctrines of *Blut und Boden* could afford little substance of traditional and historic Christian belief.

Thus instead of Gambetta's maxim of *le cléricalisme, voilà l'ennemi* there was raised the cry of *le Christianisme, voilà l'ennemi*; for the Church was confronted by a determined attempt to replace Christian doctrine by dogmas of race, blood and soil and Marxism. In the cases of Soviet Russia and Nazi Germany the conflict was plain and undeniable. In Fascist Italy, however, where the regime professed to respect historic Christianity, the alliance between Church and State was fortified by the Concordat of 1929. It is of particular interest therefore to recall Professor Binchy's verdict on the operation of its provisions in respect of education.[2] The first casualty suffered by the Church was in relation to its Boy Scouts, the *esploratori cattolici*, who were swallowed up by the 'Institute of the National Balilla for the assistance and physical and moral education of youth' (Opera Nazionale Balilla), with its blasphemous parody of the Apostles' Creed. In regard to primary education the problem was complex, for the reforms of the philosopher-minister Gentile in 1923–4 had reintroduced religious instruction into the public elementary schools, and declared that 'the teaching of Christian doctrine in the form handed down by Catholic tradition is the basis and apex of elementary education in all its branches'. But this apparently generous concession was offset by Gentile's explanation that religious instruction along traditional lines could not be restored in secondary schools, because 'when the child advances in years and increases in maturity of spirit, he will be able of his own accord to pass beyond the puerile conception of religion that has been taught him in the primary school'. The primary instruction, moreover, was usually given by the ordinary class-teacher, who must possess for this purpose an episcopal certificate. Professor Binchy emphasised that the control rested with the State, and not with the Church; and his conclusion (both reserved and cautious) was that 'in the elementary schools the church has realized its formal aim. Can one say more?'

There remained the position of the private schools conducted by teaching orders, both primary and secondary. Towards them the Gentile reforms were unfavourable; for the Ministry of Education was charged with the duty to watch over 'the private schools to safeguard the institutions of the State, public order, morality and culture'. The religious schools were thus brought under the surveillance of the Minister of Education, and suffered further disadvantages in respect of the denial of credit for the years spent in them to pupils who passed later to State higher institutions and in regard to examinations. However, the Gentile reform opened the way for recognition and pecuniary provision for schools satisfying certain conditions. Article 35 of the Concordat of 1929 further provided that 'for the secondary schools conducted by ecclesiastical or religious corporations, the institution of the state-examination under conditions of effective parity between pupils of the said schools and those of the government-controlled schools, remains unimpaired'. But the promulgation in February 1939 (immediately after the death of Pius XI) of the 'School Charter' (Carta della Scuola) seriously threatened this effective parity in the matter of examinations; and although the Church secured recognition by the State, the consequent assimilation in curriculum and text-books of ecclesiastical schools to the pattern of the State-controlled schools was a heavy price to pay for official aid and support. However, the religious position in State-controlled secondary schools was much more unsatisfactory; for although Article 36 of the Concordat provided that 'the religious instruction which is already given in the public elementary schools, shall be extended to and developed in the secondary schools, according to a programme to be settled between the Holy See and the State', in point of fact this teaching occupied precisely one hour per week only, and was not a subject of examination, though in the vast majority of cases it was given by an ecclesiastic. It was significant that the original draft Concordat, which the papacy wished to have accepted, had provided for the corporate attendance of pupils and teachers at Mass on Sundays and holy days of obligation. It was evident that the meagre prescription of one hour per week for religious instruction, in a curriculum overcrowded with examination subjects, constituted less than a Franciscan minimum of recognition of its place in secondary education. Moreover, as Pius XI remarked in *Non abbiamo bisogno*, 'even this minimum is attained amid surroundings and in an environment which do not depend on the church, but are pre-occupied by many other kinds of teaching matters, and by many other exercises in obedience to immediate superiors, who are often little or not at all favourably disposed to religion, and who sometimes exercise a directly contrary influence both by their words and by the example of their lives'.[1] The evolution of the relations between Church and State, and particularly in the field of education, was rudely interrupted by the outbreak of war and the ultimate collapse of the Fascist regime; but the history of events since the Concordat had raised grave doubts as to the adequacy of the guarantees which it afforded to the Church.

With Nazi Germany likewise the papacy endeavoured to reach a *modus vivendi*, and in its Concordat with the Hitler government in July 1933, Article 21 expressly provided that 'Catholic religious instruction in primary, vocational, secondary and higher schools is a regular subject of tuition and is to be taught in accordance with the principles of the Catholic church'. But the Article continued to insist that 'in religious instruction the patriotic, civic and social consciousness and sense of duty will be particularly stressed and cultivated, as this is generally done in the school training. The teaching programme of religious education and the selection of text-books will be settled by agreement with the higher ecclesiastical authorities. These authorities will be given the opportunity to control, in harmony with the school authorities, whether pupils are receiving religious instruction in accordance with the teaching and requirements of the Church.' Furthermore, Article 23 guaranteed 'the maintenance of the existing Catholic confessional schools and the establishment of new ones'; and Article 24 laid down that 'only members of the Catholic Church who can be trusted that they will correspond to the special requirements of a Catholic confessional school, can be employed as teachers in all Catholic primary schools', whilst Article 25 recognised that 'Religious Orders and Congregations have the right to establish and run private schools within the limits of the general legislation and conditions laid down by law'.[1] If these provisions had been sympathetically observed, the position of the Roman Catholic Church in education would have been safeguarded and a working solution established. In 1937, however, in *Mit brennender Sorge*, Pius XI voiced his disappointment and disillusion in face of 'intrigues which from the beginning had no other aim than a war of extermination', and which were motived by 'secret and open fundamental hostility to Christ and His Church'.[1]

But although the question of education was one of the nerve-centres of the contest of Church and State, it was part only of the wider issues of the relationship of the two powers, which assumed new forms in the nineteenth century. In the *Syllabus Errorum*, Item 55 denounced the opinion that 'the church should be separated from the state and the state from the church'; and much consternation was caused in the diplomatic chancelleries of Europe by the circulation at the Vatican Council in January 1870 of the draft of the schema *De Ecclesia*, consisting of fifteen chapters followed by twenty-one canons. The first chapter dealt with the Church as the mystical Body of Christ, the second with the necessity for Christianity to be practised in the Church founded by Christ, and the third affirmed the character of the Church as a *societas vera, perfecta spiritualis et supernaturalis*. Passing to consideration of the Church as a visible society, the definition noted its possession of a teaching *magisterium*, a sacerdotal *ministerium* and a hierarchical *imperium sive regimen*, with the papacy at its head; and insisted on the necessity of visible unity in the Church in communion with Rome. Therefore it followed that membership of the Church was altogether necessary, and outside the Church no one could be saved, (though allowance was made for invincible ignorance). In view of its solemn responsibilities the Church possessed the guarantee of indefectibility and infallibility, and the power of jurisdiction over all its members. The authority of the papacy, descending from the Petrine primacy, was next stated, and the necessity of the temporal dominion of the papal states as a safeguard for its exercise was emphasised. It was in the thirteenth and the two following chapters that delicate issues of the practical relationship of Church and State were treated. The divinely instituted *concordia inter Ecclesiam et societatem civilem* was declared to involve the maintenance of the traditional alliance of the two powers, and their separation was condemned. Chapter 14 sought to define the rights of the Church to exercise oversight of the policy of the State, *de jure et usu potestatis civilis secundum Ecclesiae catholicae doctrinam*, by affirming the indirect power of the papacy to pronounce upon acts of the temporal authority from the standpoint of the principles of Christian morals and justice. Finally the schema specified certain rights of the Church *vis-à-vis* the State, with particular reference to education, the exemption of the priesthood from military service, the establishment of religious orders and the right to hold property.

The assertion of a right of indirect intervention in

affairs of the civil authority caused a marked flutter in diplomatic circles. The Bavarian foreign minister, Prince Hohenlohe, brother of Cardinal Hohenlohe, was anxious to secure joint diplomatic representations of the Great Powers in order to encompass the withdrawal of the schema. Bismarck was contemptuously indifferent, and the British government was divided in sentiment; Gladstone, the prime minister, being in correspondence with Lord Acton who was in Rome for the Council and therefore sympathetic towards the Bavarian proposal; whilst the foreign minister, Lord Clarendon, was supplied with counter-arguments by the British resident in Rome, Odo Russell, who in turn was briefed by Manning, himself given papal permission to divulge the secrets of the Council for this end. But the key to the situation lay evidently with the French administration, whose troops alone prevented the kingdom of Italy from taking possession of Rome and whose decision to withdraw them would also mark the end of the Council. In Paris there developed a tug-of-war between Émile Ollivier, who became first minister of Napoleon III's Liberal Empire on 2 January 1870 and was a firm champion of non-intervention, and the foreign minister Count Daru, who was equally anxious for action. Thanks to contemporary ministerial conventions in France, it was possible for Daru to send a despatch, approved by the emperor but not submitted to Ollivier, to the French ambassador to the Vatican for presentation to Cardinal Antonelli, papal secretary of state, on 20 February, protesting against the invasion of the rights of the civil power by the schema *De Ecclesia*. The actual presentation of this despatch, however, was respited by order of a ministerial council on the 21st, and its contents were subjected to revision by Ollivier in such a way as to draw its teeth. Daru and the emperor, meanwhile, were under continual pressure from the minority group of French bishops at the Council, who regarded the definition of papal infallibility as inopportune, but preferred to secure the rejection of the schema by diplomatic action on the part of Napoleon's administration rather than to oppose it outright in the conciliar sessions. But a half-hearted despatch was worse than inaction, and Antonelli judged rightly that the French intervention lacked force; and although the division of opinion in the administration continued to encourage hopes of action, the resignation of Daru on 11 April resolved the conflict, and was saluted by the sending of a private telegram to Rome on that same evening, *Daru se retire, Ollivier remplace, Concile libre.*[1]

The assertion of the rights of the Church and the revival of a vigorous Church-consciousness were not confined to the Roman Church and to Continental Europe. In the British Isles also, similar manifestations were occurring. In particular the Disruption in the Church of Scotland presented a direct answer on the part of the seceders to the alleged infringement by the State of the sovereignty and independence of the Church. The secession had its origin in the oft-disputed question of rights of patronage; for, notwithstanding the incorporation of an Act for the Security of the Church of Scotland in the Act of Union of England and Scotland in 1707, the parliament of the United Kingdom by an Act of 1712 (10 Anne c. 10 & 21) restored lay patronage in the Church of Scotland. During the following three-quarters of a century the exercise of the right reduced the concurrence or assent of the congregation to the appointment of a minister to a mere formality, so that in 1782 there was even a movement for its abolition, but the General Assembly voted that it was 'agreeable to the immemorial and constitutional practice of this Church and ought to be continued'. With the religious revival within Presbyterianism at the beginning of the nineteenth century, however, there came a demand for the restoration of the reality of the 'call' to the parish, as a means of improving the intellectual and spiritual standards of the ministry and preventing the intrusion of unworthy ministers. In 1832 the General Assembly received eleven several petitions to this end, but resolved by 127 votes to 85 to take no action. The question was raised again in the two following years; and in 1834 the reformers by a majority of 184 to 138 secured recognition of the right of a congregation to exclude by a majority vote a candidate whom it deemed unsuitable. An occasion for testing the strength of the weapon thus forged was furnished almost immediately by the nomination on the part of Lord Kinnoul in August 1834 of Mr Robert Young to the parish of Auchterarder, which thus became a *cause célèbre* in the history of the Kirk. By a singular irony, the presbytery of Auchterarder had been responsible for the most radical of the petitions to the General Assembly in 1832; and the congregation now refused its concurrence by 286 out of 330 male heads of families, with the support of the presbytery. The presentee took his case to law, when eight out of thirteen judges of the Court of Session held the refusal to be illegal; and more unfortunately still, the president in giving judgement permitted himself to use language of extreme provocation, by his observation 'that our Saviour is Head of the Kirk of Scotland in any temporal or legislative or judicial sense, is a position which I can dignify by no other name than absurdity; the Parliament is the temporal head of the Church,...from whose Acts alone it exists as the National Church and derives all its powers'. Although the statement from a legal standpoint was sound, theologically it was obnoxious; and in 1838 the General Assembly by 183 to 142 votes affirmed that, 'while they unqualifiedly acknowledge the exclusive jurisdiction of the civil courts in regard to the civil rights and emoluments secured by law to the Church and the ministers thereof, and will ever give and inculcate obedience to their decisions thereanent, [they] do resolve that...in all matters touching the doctrine, discipline and government of the Church, her Judicatories possess an exclusive jurisdiction founded on the Word of God....And they do further resolve that this spiritual jurisdiction and the supremacy and sole headship of the Lord Jesus Christ, on which it depends, they will assert and at all hazards defend.' The case was carried on appeal to the House of Lords, which allowed to the presbytery a right to reject a patron's nominee only on the grounds of heresy, ignorance or immorality; in reply to which the General Assembly, whilst accepting the verdict so far as concerned the temporalties of a benefice, reasserted the right of the congregation to refuse the spiritual ministrations of a minister whom it had rejected. Not even a compromise proposed by the Melbourne administration, in the form of a Bill giving to the presbytery the right of decision on specific objections made to a presentee but disallowing merely general objections, was acceptable to the Assembly.

Into the midst of this smouldering fire there came another disputed case of patronage, when the Trustees of Lord Fife, as patrons of the living of Marnoch in the presbytery of Strathbogie, presented Mr John Edwards; to whom in turn the congregation refused its call by 261 male heads of families out of 300. When Edwards on his part appealed to the Court of Session, it required the presbytery to receive him on probation, and they consented to do this by 7 votes to 4. Thereupon the standing committee of the General Assembly of 1839 retaliated by suspending the seven presbyters who had accepted the court's decision. Worse was to follow at Marnoch, where Edwards' installation was effected by force; and the General Assembly in 1841 formally deposed from the ministry the seven presbyters who had ordained and supported Edwards. When a further attempt to reach a political compromise failed, secession was evidently near at hand. In 1842 the Assembly carried by 216 votes to 147 a resolution for the abolition of the right of patronage; and followed this by adopting by 241 votes to 110 the formal statement known as the Claim, Declaration and Protest. This document recognised 'the absolute jurisdiction of the civil courts...in relation to all temporalties conferred by the state on the church', repudiated the attempt to 'intrude ministers on reclaiming congregations', declared 'that all and whatsoever acts of the parliament of Great Britain, passed without the consent of the church and nation, in alteration of or derogatory to the government, discipline, rights and privileges of the church, ...as also all and whatsoever sentences of courts in contravention of the same government, discipline, rights and privileges, are and shall in themselves be null and void and of no legal force or effect'; and finally called 'the Christian people of this kingdom and all the Churches of the Reformation throughout the whole world, who hold the great doctrine of the sole headship of the Lord Jesus Christ over His Church, to witness that it is for their adherence to that doctrine...that this Church is subjected to hardship, and that the rights so sacredly pledged and secured to her are put in peril'. In the following year on 24 May 1843, the Free Church of

Scotland came into being by the secession of 474 ministers.

Professor Laski in his younger and more regenerate days applauded the principle of the Disruption and discerned a kinship of spirit betwixt it and the contemporary Tractarian revival in the Church of England. 'It is not a little curious that more attention should not have been paid to the remarkable analogy between the Oxford Movement and the Disruption of 1843 in the established Church of Scotland. Each was essentially an anti-Erastian movement. It was against an all-absorptive state that each group of men was contending. There is a striking temporal parallel between the two movements. That of Oxford in the narrower sense begins in 1833 and ends with the conversion of Newman in 1845; that of which Chalmers was the distinguished leader, begins in 1834 with the abolition by the General Assembly of lay patronage and ends in 1843 with the secession of those who refused to accept what they term an invasion of the peculiar province of the church by the state. In each case, as was well enough admitted by contemporaries, the attempt was made...to work out a doctrine of the church, which, neglecting the state, gave the church the general organization of a perfect society.'[1] The protest of the Tractarians indeed was voiced *more Anglicano* in muted tones, and the reverberations of John Keble's Assize sermon were more muffled than those of Thomas Chalmers' philippics. Nor were the political campaigns which resulted in the disestablishment of the Irish Church in 1870 and the Welsh Church in 1914 the effects of High Church protests against the fetters of the State, nor of anti-clerical sentiment on the part of Parliament, but of Nonconformist agitation for complete equality with the Anglican churches. Nevertheless, the chief contribution of the Oxford Movement was its re-statement of the doctrine of the sovereignty and independence of the Church. As Dr Brilioth remarked succinctly, 'the great discovery of the Oxford Movement was that the Church was a living organism'.

As a result of this revival of a vigorous Church-consciousness, the pontificate of Leo XIII witnessed the issue of a notable series of Encyclicals, defining the nature of the Church and its relationship to the modern State. In *Immortale Dei* of 1885, the pope laid down as an axiom that the State 'is clearly bound to satisfy its many and great duties towards God by the public profession of religion', as an obligation imposed by nature and reason as well as by revelation. Further, 'states cannot without crime act as though God did not exist, nor cast off the care of religion as alien to them or useless, or out of several kinds of religion adopt whichever they please'. For, 'God has divided the charge of the human race between two powers, the ecclesiastical and the civil, the one being set over divine and the other over human things. Each is supreme in its kind; each has fixed limits within which it is contained, and those limits are defined by the nature and special object of each; so that there is, as it were, a circle marked out, within which each acts by its own right.' Since, however, there are evidently certain 'mixed matters' which fall legitimately within the province of both powers, God 'has in due order arranged the course of each in right relation to the other'; and he has done this 'by having regard to the nature of each power and taking account of the relative excellence and nobility of their purpose; for one of them has for its proximate and chief object the comforts of this mortal life, the other, the everlasting joys of heaven. Whatever, therefore, in human things is in any way sacred; whatever pertains to the salvation of souls or to the worship of God, either in its own nature or by reason of the end to which it is referred; all this is subject to the power and judgment of the Church.' In dealing with these issues, however, 'there are times when another method of concord is available for peace and liberty', namely by the conclusion of Concordats between the papacy and particular States. The pope further traced the origin of the evils afflicting and perverting the modern State to 'that fatal and deplorable passion for innovation which was aroused in the sixteenth century'; from which there had ensued the practice of contemporary States and also the theory that the State 'does not hold itself bound to inquire which of the many religions is the only true one, nor to prefer one religion to the rest and to shew it special favour, but rather to give equal rights to all religions'. In such States, 'to the Catholic religion is assigned only a position equal or inferior to that of alien societies'.[1]

There lies the rub. For the Christian Church in face of the totalitarian State is divided into many fragments, not all of which find it easy to preserve the unity of the Spirit in the bond of peace; and therefrom arises the question whether any church can claim for itself the totalitarian authority asserted by some temporal powers. The difficulty of the Roman Church in this respect was frankly stated by Professor Binchy.

The Catholic Church's attitude towards religious toleration may be 'a byword and a shaking of the head' to all champions of unrestricted freedom of thought, as well as a 'hard saying' to many others who have much sympathy with the Church's general programme; but friend and foe alike must admit that it is the only logical conclusion from the premisses on which the Catholic religion is based. The Church could only surrender that conclusion by surrendering its fundamental claim to being, by divine institution and guidance, the sole and infallible repository of religious truth. Once these premisses are accepted, as all Catholics must accept them, it follows necessarily that other denominations which reject its authority and some at least of its proclaimed dogmas, are in error. Shall error be allowed to propagate itself freely and to attract souls away from the truth? The Church's answer is that of St Augustine: *Quae enim est pejor mors animae quam libertas erroris?* Accordingly it repudiates the idea of parity of cults, of religious liberty in the sense of freedom for other denominations to proselytize Catholics, as an attempt to equate error with truth. But this does not mean, as is often stated, that it denies the liberty of the individual conscience. When Pius XI distinguished 'freedom of consciences' from 'freedom of conscience', he summarized neatly the traditional Catholic doctrine. Faith is a gift of God; it cannot be expected from him who does not possess it, and so the Canon Law lays down expressly: *Ad amplexandam fidem Catholicam nemo invitus cogatur*. And in the domain of practice, while denying the right of other religions to be placed *pari passu* with itself, it does not seek to prevent secular governments from tolerating them. Liberty of consciences therefore, which in practice means toleration for other cults, but not liberty of conscience, if this is held to cover 'unrestricted freedom of discussion, including those forms of discussion which can easily deceive the good faith of simple hearers and thus become disguised forms of propaganda, harmful to the religion of the State'.[1]

The issue was raised in an acute and controversial form by Item 77 of the *Syllabus Errorum*, which denounced the perverse opinion that 'in this present age it is no longer expedient that the Catholic religion should be treated as the sole State religion and that any other forms of religious worship should be excluded'. Further, Item 78 continued by reprobating the contention that 'those States, nominally Catholic, which have legally enacted that immigrants be permitted to have free exercise of their own particular religion, are to be praised'. The statement of these propositions embarrassed gravely the Liberal Catholics of France and other countries, who had been striving for a reconciliation of Rome with the principles of contemporary States. Accordingly Bishop Dupanloup of Orleans set forward an interpretation of their purport by elaborating the difference between *thesis* and *hypothesis* in his *Lettre sur la Convention du 15 Septembre et sur l'Encyclique du 9 Décembre*. The history of this manifesto has been recently traced in detail by Canon R. Aubert, with especial emphasis upon the distinction between *thesis* and *hypothesis*.[1] The writer observes that, though of long standing recognition in rhetoric, it was of recent introduction into theology, particularly with relation to modern liberties, where it made its first appearance in an article in the *Civiltà Cattolica* of 2 October 1863. In a further article on 6 December, as the bishop of Poitiers was informed, 'la distinction entre la thèse et l'hypothèse,...n'est pas seulement une idée, mais aussi une formule donnée par le Saint-Père, avec qui les rédacteurs ont eu à ce sujet de très longues conversations'. Dupanloup's cardinal point was to insist on the necessity not to confuse 'deux ordres distincts: l'ordre relatif et l'ordre absolu, confondre ce qu'on est convenu depuis quelque temps d'appeler la thèse et l'hypothèse'. The propositions stated in the *Syllabus* represented the thesis, that is the ideal and absolute; and did not in any wise prevent Rome from recognising the hypothesis, namely the actual and relative, and therefore from making agreements with modern States whose practice tolerated declensions from the ideal in various spheres of public life. So long as these concordats did not elevate to the status of principle such matters as religious toleration, the equality of Rome with other churches, and the allowance to other churches of freedom of propaganda and printing, the papacy could accept their concessions, because of the hardness of men's hearts and the untowardness of the times. 'Il y a pour le pape et l'Église un autre idéal, et il ne faut jamais leur demander de transformer en vérités absolues les nécessités relatives, d'ériger des faits regrettables, des divisions malheureuses mais tolérées, en principes dogmatiques.' The relief which the brochure brought to many consciences was testified by its tremendous success and by the messages of congratulation received. Montalembert, however, was doubtful of its power to convince. 'Quant à la justification de l'Encyclique, malgré la place honorable qui m'y est assignée, je n'y puis voir qu'un subterfuge très éloquent.' Canon Aubert also is constrained to admit that incontestably Dupanloup 'esquivait certaines difficultés qui pouvaient être opposées par l'esprit moderne à quelques passages de *Quanta cura* et du *Syllabus*'. French opinion indeed was considerably divided; but what mattered most was not the reception accorded to the pamphlet in Paris, but the verdict in Rome at the Vatican.

There Pio Nono, in conversation with the vicar-general of Mgr Pie, bishop of Poitiers, *à propos* of Montalembert's address to the Liberal Catholic Congress at Malines in 1863 and the question of 'the great principle of freedom of conscience', had remarked that 'l'Église n'admettra jamais comme un bien et un principe que l'on puisse prêcher l'erreur et l'hérésie à des peuples catholiques. Le pape veut bien la liberté de conscience en Suède et en

Russie; mais il ne la veut pas en principe: il la veut comme un moyen que la Providence pourrait susciter de répandre la vérité dans ces régions.'[1] Dupanloup was, therefore, excusably anxious to secure a commendation from the pope; and the first reports of the reception of his brochure in the curia were most favourable. But Louis Veuillot was spending that winter in Rome, and a tug-of-war ensued between his friends and those of the bishop at the Vatican. Twice Pius IX suggested changes in the draft submitted to him, until finally Dupanloup's allies, with the help of the flexible Latin tongue, hammered out a form of sound words by which the pope expressed his hope that Dupanloup 'would devote himself the more energetically and diligently to explaining to his people the true meaning of the Encyclical as he had more vehemently refuted the calumnious interpretations imposed on it'.[2] As Mgr Mercurelli, who had composed the letter, justly affirmed, 'ce n'est pas une lettre d'approbation du principe, mais c'est une lettre d'éloges'.

The application of the principle of the hypothesis to contemporary States may be seen in the Constitutions of Austria and of Eire. The Austrian Constitution of 1934 in its 27th Article granted to all citizens 'full freedom of religious conviction and of conscience, as well as the freedom to practice their religion at home or publicly'; and Article 29 further stated that 'the Catholic Church and other Churches and religious bodies recognized by law enjoy a status regulated by public law', embracing 'the exclusive right for all its members to practice their religion collectively and publicly'. In regard to sects not legally recognised as religious bodies, their adherents notwithstanding 'can associate with a view of regular worship or with a view of any other manifestation of their belief'. In the Constitution of Eire of 1937, Article 44 stated that 'the State acknowledges that the homage of public worship is due to almighty God', recognised 'the special position of the Holy, Catholic, Apostolic and Roman Church as the guardian of the Faith professed by the great majority of the citizens'; and also recognised 'the Church of Ireland, the Presbyterian Church in Ireland, the Methodist Church in Ireland, the Religious Society of Friends in Ireland, as well as the Jewish congregations and the other religious denominations existing in Ireland'. To all citizens the Constitution guaranteed 'freedom of conscience and the free profession and practice of religion'.[1] In these countries therefore acceptance of the *hypothesis* (albeit without renunciation of the *thesis*) constituted a satisfactory working agreement. On the other hand in the Concordat with Spain of 1953, Article 6 declared that 'the profession and practice of the Catholic religion, which is the religion of the Spanish state, will enjoy official protection'; and in regard to other churches, whilst 'no one shall be disturbed by reason of his religious beliefs or the private observance of his form of worship', yet 'ceremonies and public manifestations, other than those of the religion of the state, are not permitted'.

Here the *thesis* has swallowed up the *hypothesis*; though the reason may lie in the policy of the Spanish government and not in the demand of the Vatican. In Spain, therefore, the right of public worship is allowed only to the Roman Catholic Church, and other Christian churches must be content with a purely private exercise of their rites.

There is the crux. In the face of contemporary totalitarian regimes the Christian Church, and also the several churches, must demand full liberty of worship, preaching, teaching and means of propaganda. Mere permission to assemble for public worship is insufficient without the accompanying freedom to teach and publish. Hence the prominence of the question of education as the nerve-centre of the present-day relationship of Church and State, and the general recognition of its cruciality for the Church. Professor Binchy, as has already been noted, is persuaded that even 'before the advent of the totalitarian systems, the school-question represented perhaps the most sensitive point of the relations between Church and State. The rise of the modern secularist State, among whose functions universal education is of primary importance, precipitated a quarrel with the Church which still awaits a satisfactory solution.'[1] Indeed, Dr J. H. Oldham issued the pregnant warning a quarter of a century ago that 'it may well be that the main conflict between Christian faith and the secular interpretation of life will have to be waged in the field of public education. The Church will have won little in obtaining liberty to preach and to conduct its own worship and services, if the whole weight of a public system of education is directed towards inculcating in the impressionable mind of youth beliefs about the world and man and conduct which are incompatible with the Christian understanding of life.'[1] Similarly Professor H. G. Wood has written that 'today the grand question is, in what ways and on what conditions should Church and State co-operate in the field of education'; and has answered that 'in the realm of education, which...must be either the meeting place or the battlefield for Church and State in the modern world, co-operation with the State is desirable, if it be possible, and such co-operation may involve State support of the Church in religious education'.[2]

But, if the Christian Church is to make a just and fair concordat with the State, or, where this is impossible, to stand firmly in defence of liberty of conscience, it must accept the same principle in the relationship of the several churches with each other. As Dr Wood has further remarked, 'the Christian as such is committed to demand from the State the fullest measure of religious liberty for others as well as for himself, and that not as a matter of expediency, but on grounds of principle, because without freedom of worship and freedom of thought it is impossible to fulfil God's purpose for man in creation'.[3] Thus Montalembert succinctly observed to the Liberal Catholic Congress at Malines in 1863, 'L'inquisiteur espagnol qui disait à l'hérétique: La vérité ou la mort: m'est aussi odieux que le terroriste français disant a mon grandpère: la liberté, la fraternité, ou la mort.' Experience and conviction have combined to lead most churches to accept the principle of freedom of conscience, not as an expedient but as a rule. It may well be that the distinction between *thesis* and *hypothesis* will prove a satisfactory means whereby the Roman Church can adjust itself to modern conditions, provided it is fully accepted and applied as in the constitutions of Austria and Eire. But religious liberty finds its surest basis and charter only in the principles of the Gospel. In his Hulsean Lectures on *Persecution and Tolerance*, delivered in 1894, when the Liberal State was still enjoying the Indian summer of its prosperity, Mandell Creighton issued the prescient warning that 'I do not know that the tolerance which is now praised by the world is very firmly established. It rests at present mainly on an equilibrium of forces which might easily be upset. There is always a temptation to the possessors of power—be they an individual, an institution, or a class—to use it selfishly or harshly. Liberty is a tender plant and needs jealous watching. It is always unsafe in the world, and is only secure under the guardianship of the Church; for the Church possesses the knowledge of man's eternal destiny, which alone can justify his claim to freedom.' But the Church can only justify the claim thus made in its behalf, if it holds unswervingly to tolerance as an integral element of the Gospel. For, as Creighton further affirmed: 'Tolerance is not merely a negative virtue. It is needful on the part of the Church as an organized body; for only by its liberal exercise can the sincerity of its individual members be preserved. No educator can discharge his task unless he encourages frankness, outspokenness and sincerity amongst those whom he undertakes to teach. The Church, as the divinely-appointed educator of mankind, must cherish these qualities. Tolerance is needful to the individual; for it is the expression of that reverence for others, which forms a great part of the lesson which Christ came to teach him.'[1]

NOTES

PAGE 1

1 Melchior Cano, *op. cit.* lib. xi, cap. 2 (*Opera*, 2 vols., 1776, vol. II, pp. 2–3).

PAGE 2

1 P. Polman, *L'Élément Historique dans la Controverse Religieuse du XVIème Siècle* (Louvain University Dissertations, series II, tom. 23, Gembloux, 1932), p. 201.

PAGE 4

1 A. Rébelliau, *Bossuet, Historien du Protestantisme* (Paris, 1891), p. 98.

2 A. Godeau, *Histoire de l'Église* (3 vols., 4th edition, Paris, 1672), Preface.

PAGE 5

1 A. Natalis, *Selecta Historiae Ecclesiasticae Capita* (2nd edition, Paris, 1679), vol. I, Praefatio, p. 284.

2 Rébelliau, *op. cit.* quoting Lamy, *Entretiens sur les Sciences* (1684).

3 L. E. Du Pin, *Bibliothèque des Auteurs Ecclésiastiques du XVIIème Siècle*, I, Avertissement.

4 Jean Mabillon, *Traité des Études Monastiques*, seconde partie (Paris, 1691), pp. 303–4. Cette étude est beaucoup plus avantageuse que la plupart du monde ne s'imagine, et...il y a des très fortes raisons de s'y appliquer, surtout à l'étude de l'Histoire Ecclésiastique. Car il est certain que sans cette étude on ne peut avoir une parfaite intelligence des Pères, ni de la Théologie, et que c'est par là qu'on apprend non seulement la morale par les exemples, mais aussi les dogmes de notre religion....En effet j'ai appris d'un des plus beaux esprits de ce siècle, qui a été engagé

autrefois dans l'hérésie par sa naissance, que rien n'avait plus contribué à se désabuser de son erreur, que la lecture de l'histoire ecclésiastique.

PAGE 9

1 Eusebius, *H.E.* I, I, 3.

PAGE 10

1 C. H. Firth, *A Plea for the Historical Teaching of History* (Oxford, 1904), pp. 8–9.

PAGE 11

1 E. T. Merrill, *Essays in Early Christian History* (London, 1924), p. 4.

PAGE 12

1 M. Bloch, *The Historian's Craft* (Eng. trans. by P. Putnam, Manchester, 1954), pp. 4–5, 31. *Apologie pour l'Histoire, ou Métier d'historien* (Paris, 1949).

2 Bloch, *op. cit.* p. 36.

3 Mabillon, *Traité des Études Monastiques*, seconde partie, pp. 315–27.

PAGE 15

1 J. H. Newman, Introduction to the *Essay on Development* (2nd edition, London, 1846), p. 5.

PAGE 16

1 Boswell, *Life of Johnson* (ed. G. B. Hill and L. Powell, Oxford, 1934), II, 409; III, 197.
2 C. C. J. Webb, *Religion and the Thought of Today* (Oxford, 1929), p. 13.

PAGE 17

1 Baronius, *Annales Ecclesiastici* (10 vols., Antwerp, 1610), I, Praefatio.
2 Acts ii. 22–4, 36.

PAGE 18

1 J. B. Bury, *Selected Essays* (ed. H. W. V. Temperley), pp. 4, 17.

2 R. G. Collingwood, 'Human Nature and Human History', *Proceedings of the British Academy*, vol. XXII, 1936, p. 12.

PAGE 19

1 Bloch, *op. cit.* pp. 14, 17, 103, 151 (Engl. trans.). Le mot de Bayle demeure toujours juste. 'Jamais on n'objectera rien qui vaille contre cette vérité que César a battu Pompée, et que, dans quelque sorte de principe qu'on veuille passer en disputant, on ne trouvera guère de choses plus inébranlables que cette proposition: César et Pompée ont existé et n'ont pas été une simple modification de l'âme de ceux qui ont écrit leur vie.' Il est vrai: s'il ne devait subsister comme assuré, que quelques faits de ce type, dépourvue d'explication, l'histoire se réduirait à une suite de notations grossières, sans grande valeur intellectuelle. Par bonheur, tel n'est point le cas (p. 48).

PAGE 21

1 Helen Gardner, *The Limits of Literary Criticism* (Riddell Lectures, no. 28, Oxford, 1946), pp. 17–18.

2 *Ibid.* p. 25.

PAGE 22

1 *Ibid.* pp. 33, 36–7, 39.

2 E. Auerbach, *Mimesis: The Representation of Reality in Western Literature* (Eng. trans. by W. R. Trask, Princeton, 1953), chs. 1–2.

3 In W. D. Davies and D. Daube, *The Background of the New Testament and its Eschatology* (Cambridge, 1956), pp. 212, 213, 215, 219–20.

PAGE 24

1 F. J. Foakes-Jackson, *Eusebius Pamphili* (Cambridge, 1933), p. 73.

NOTES

PAGE 25

1 Baronius, *Annales*, Praefatio, p. 2.

2 Gibbon, *The Decline and Fall of the Roman Empire* (ed. J. B. Bury), vol. II, p. 26; *Memoirs of my Life* (ed. G. B. Hill), p. 68.

PAGE 26

1 Eusebius, *H.E.* v, 5, 1–6, for the Thundering Legion; 7, 1–6 for Irenaeus.

PAGE 27

1 C. V. Langlois and C. Seignobos, *Introduction aux Études Historiques* (Paris, 1898), pp. 177–8.

2 F. R. Tennant, *Philosophy of the Sciences*, p. 121.

3 N. H. Baynes, *Constantine the Great and the Christian Church* (British Academy Lecture, 1922), p. 9.

PAGE 28

1 F. J. Foakes-Jackson, *A History of Church History* (Cambridge, 1939), p. 5.

2 F. M. Powicke, *History, Freedom and Religion* (Riddell Lectures, Oxford, 1938), p. 16; I. Berlin, *Historical Inevitability* (Auguste Comte Memorial Lecture, no. 1, London, 1953), p. 6; J. N. Figgis, *Christianity and History* (London, 1905), p. 62.

PAGE 29

1 Bury, *op. cit.* pp. 37, 64; Baynes, *op. cit.* p. 3.

2 Tennant, *op. cit.* pp. 93, 116.

3 Powicke, *op. cit.* p. 5; Webb, *op. cit.* p. 16.

PAGE 30

1 Tertullian, *Ad Nationes* I, 8.

2 Berlin, *op. cit.* pp. 55–6.

3 C. H. Dodd, *History and the Gospel* (London, 1938), pp. 29–30.

PAGE 31

1 L. Hodgson, *For Faith and Freedom* (Gifford Lectures, I, Oxford, 1956), p. 237.

2 Tennant, *op. cit.* p. 119.

PAGE 32

1 A. E. Taylor, *The Faith of a Moralist* (1930), II, pp. 128–9.

PAGE 34

1 *Obedience in Church and State.* Three Political Tracts by Stephen Gardiner (ed. Pierre Janelle, Cambridge, 1930). *De Vera Obedientia Oratio*, p. 136. The reference is to Eusebius, *H.E.* II, I, 6, citing Clement of Alexandria, *Hypotyposes.*

PAGE 36

1 Luther, *Omnia Opera* (7 vols., Wittenberg), vol. I, pp. 311, 318, 322.

2 Calvin, *Institutes* (1559 edition), book IV, cap. VI. *De primatu Romanae sedis.* Section I.

PAGE 39

1 I Clement, v. Λάβωμεν τῆς γενεᾶς ἡμῶν τὰ γενναῖα ὑποδείγματα. διὰ ζῆλον καὶ φθόνον οἱ μέγιστοι καὶ δικαιότατοι στύλοι ἐδιώχθησαν καὶ ἕως θανάτου ἤθλησαν. Λάβωμεν πρὸ ὀφθαλμῶν ἡμῶν τοὺς ἀγαθοὺς ἀποστόλους, Πέτρον, ὃς διὰ ζῆλον ἄδικον οὐχ ἕνα οὐδὲ δύο, ἀλλὰ πλείονας ὑπήνεγκεν πόνους καὶ οὕτω μαρτυρήσας ἐπορεύθη εἰς τὸν ὀφειλόμενον τόπον τῆς δόξης. διὰ ζῆλον καὶ ἔριν Παῦλος ὑπομονῆς βραβεῖον ὑπέδειξεν.

2 Ignatius, *To the Romans*, iv. Οὐχ ὡς Πέτρος καὶ Παῦλος διατάσσομαι ὑμῖν. ἐκεῖνοι ἀπόστολοι, ἐγὼ κατάκριτος. ἐκεῖνοι ἐλεύθεροι, ἐγὼ δὲ μέχρι νῦν δοῦλος.

3 J. B. Lightfoot, *Apostolic Fathers*, part I, vol. I, pp. 69–70; part II, vol. II, p. 186; P. Batiffol, *L'Église Naissante*, p. 146.

PAGE 41

1 *Operum Johannis Driedonis*...tomus primus (Louvain, 1582), pp. 224v–225. *Latomi*...*Opera*, quae praecipue adversus horum temporum haereses...conscripsit (Louvain, 1550), pp. 82v–83.

2 *Hierarchiae Ecclesiasticae Assertio per Albertum Pighium*, ff. 8r, 12r: Cui [Ecclesiae Romanae] ut omnium maximae et principalissimae, necesse sit universam ecclesiam conformari et consentire in fide. 125r: Irenaeus...adversos haereticos tamen, ut inefficacem aut infinitum per universas ecclesias discursum fugiens, unam ex omnibus et pro omnibus profert maximam, ut dicit, antiquissimam abque omnibus cognitam Romanam Ecclesiam, atque ejus fidem proferens, confundit universos, qui Scripturis confundi non possent, haereticos.

3 F. Feuardent, *Irenaei Opera* (Paris, 1576), p. 161 (*b*): Multis iisque gravissimis verbis hoc loco, totoque capite, docet beatus Martyr Romanam Ecclesiam caput esse et regulam omnium aliarum. P. 162 (*a*): Ad hanc subjungit Ecclesiam Romanam videlicet, non ad urbis amplitudinem, populorum frequentiam, censorum gravitatem, senatusque statuta; non ad fortissimos ejus exercitus, gloriosos de toto orbe triumphos, imperii culmen, non denique ad Caesarem majestatem;...sed ad hanc Ecclesiam, in qua sedit vertex Apostolorum....Necesse est quia a Deo Optimo Maximo constitutum, non tantum Europeam, Africanam, Alexandrinam, Asiaticam et Orientalem Ecclesiam, sed omnem, hoc est, qui sunt undique fideles, ut membra cum capite convenire, nec latum unguem ab ejus communione discedere. Et vero id necesse est, ait, duplici de causa; altera, propter potentiorem principalitatem, seu locum, gradumque principem in jurisdictione et authoritate, quem prae caeteris omnibus obtinet; altera, quia in ea semper conservata est, ea quae est ab Apostolis verae fidei et pietatis syncerae traditio.

4 M. Flacius Illyricus, *Centuriata*, cent. III, cap. IV, col. 64: Ignatius in Epigrapha Epistolae ad Romanos eam Ecclesiam appellat eminentia dignam. Verum nihil aliud ab

Ignatio assertum est, quam esse excellentem Ecclesiam. Nam ad Romanam Ecclesiam omnes alias in toto orbe terrarum esse alligatas, et episcopum ejus loci esse Oecumenicum, qui errare non potest, et cui omnes necesse sit subesse, neque Ignatius neque alii hujus aetatis scriptores habent. Novitatem deinde quandam et illud resipere quibusdam videri posset quod in exemplaribus Irenaei, qualia nunc habemus, extat Libro tertio, capite tertio: 'Ad hanc ecclesiam propter potentiorem principalitatem, necesse est omnem convenire ecclesiam; hoc est, eos qui sunt undique fideles, in qua semper ab his qui sunt undique conservata est ea quae est ab Apostolis traditio.' Sed haec sententia tantum de consensu in doctrina ab Apostolis tradita loquitur, sicut ex contextu Irenaei manifestum est.

PAGE 42

1 W. L. Knox, 'Irenaeus, *Adv. Haer.* III, 3, 2', *Journal of Theological Studies*, vol. XLVII, no. 187–8 (July–October, 1946), pp. 180–4; T. G. Jalland, *The Church and the Papacy*, pp. 109–15.

2 J. Forget, 'Le Témoinage de S. Irénée en faveur de la Primauté Romaine', *Revue d'Histoire Ecclésiastique*, vol. XXIII (1927), pp. 276–7; and *Ephemerides Theologicae Lovanienses*, vol. V (1928), pp. 437–61.

PAGE 43

1 Pierre Nautin, '*Irénée: Adv. Haer.* III, 3, 2. L'Église de Rome ou l'église universelle?', *Revue de l'Histoire des Religions*, vol. CLI, no. 1 (January–March, 1957), pp. 37–78. I owe this reference to Dr Henry Chadwick.

2 Luther, *Omnia Opera*, I, pp. 244*a*, 246*b*.

3 *Ibid.* pp. 244*a*, 247*a*, 331*a*. Luther cited several of Cyprian's Letters: nos. XLVII, Hartel, II, p. 605; XLVIII, p. 608; LI, p. 613; LII, p. 616; LVIII, p. 666; LXVI, p. 717; LXVII, p. 735.

PAGE 44

1 *Ibid.* p. 250*b*.

2 Calvin, *Institutio Christianae Religionis* (1559), book IV, cap. VI: De primatu Romanae Sedis, 4.

3 Flacius Illyricus, *Ecclesiastica Historia...secundum singulas Centurias* [Magdeburg Centuries] (Basle, 1562), cent. III, cap. VII, ff. 171–2. Quid Cyprianus de primatu Romanae Ecclesiae senserit, ex his apparet, quod Cornelium fratrem et sacerdotem appellat....Et quod...satis graviter Cornelium reprehendit, quod minis et terroribus haereticorum commotus, literas ab eis accepisset et non potius eos remisisset ad suum episcopum in Africam; cum statutum sit ab omnibus episcopis, ut uniuscuiusque causa illic audiatur, ubi crimen admissum esset. Et asserit auctoritatem episcoporum in Africa non esse minorem quam eorum qui Romae causam illorum cognovissent....

Quod vero Cyprianus...Romanam Ecclesiam cathedram Petri et Ecclesiam principalem appellat, unde sacerdotalis exorta sit unitas. Eo sensu dicitur, quod Romana Ecclesia alias sit exhortata ad consociationem mutuam et quod in ea re prae caeteris laborarit, non quod iure aliquo divino prima et caput aliarum sit constituta....

Nam consociationem illam omnium Ecclesiarum et episcoporum in consensione doctrinae et disciplinae ecclesiasticae, vocat unitatem.

Cyprian, *Epistola* LVIIII: ad Petri cathedram adque ad ecclesiam principalem, unde unitas sacerdotalis exorta est (Hartel, II, p. 683).

PAGE 47

1 *Cypriani Opera* (Geneva, 1593): In eo fallitur Pamelius, quod scopum Cypriani relinquens ad primatum Pontificium respicit. Atqui non de primatu, sed de unitate Ecclesiae agit Cyprianus (p. 304*b*, note 9). Quaeritur, cum Apostoli sint Petro aequales, cur uni Petro dictum sit, tibi dabo claves regni caelorum etc. Respondet Cyprianus, *ut una Ecclesia monstretur*: Pamelius vero, *ut primatus Episcopo Romano tribuatur*. Ista certe non modo

diversa, sed ex diametro opposita videntur. Nam si Ecclesia una est, omnes in ea pastores pari consortio honoris et potestatis praediti sunt; contra, si potestas huius major, illius minor, Ecclesia scinditur. Primatum constitue, Ecclesiam dividis; nam ut una, ita unus est episcopatus et indivisus est, cuius a singulis in solidum pars tenetur (*ibid.*). Glossema illud igitur Hosii, ex margine in textum irrepsit, ut ex verborum serie manifeste apparet (p. 305 *a*). Codex meus cum Gratiano legit *super unum aedificat Ecclesiam*. *Idem*, ut et Gratianus, reliqua, *et illi pascendas mandat oves suas*, omittunt.

2 Episcopos esse jure divino a Christo institutos....Et tamen si solus Pontifex immediate habet potestatem a Christo, et nulli alii, et illud tantum est de jure divino, quod est immediate institutum a Christo; ergo solus Papa est episcopus jure divino (*Concilium Tridentinum*, tom. IX, p. 50, line 26 *seq.*).

PAGE 48

1 *Ibid.* tom. II, p. 733, line 30, pp. 734–5, line 1 *seq.*

2 *Ibid.* tom. IX, p. 155, line 3, and p. 158, line 15.

3 *Ibid.* p. 171, line 3. Cyprian, *Ep.* III.

4 *Ibid.* p. 186, line 5.

PAGE 49

1 *Ibid.* p. 191, line 13 *seq.*: Ibi enim dum dicitur: Episcopatus unus est, cujus a singulis pars in solidum tenetur, pro cujus intellectu ponderanda est illa dictio, *in solidum*, quae ex sua natura requirit concursum saltem duorum ad eandem rem, ut per Legislat: in toto titulo ff: de duobus reis. Ponderanda est etiam illa dictio, *tenetur*, quae debet intelligi diversa ratione sive respectu; nam una et eadem res non potest teneri a pluribus in solidum eadem ratione sive eodem respectu ob repugnantiam naturae et legis, ut inquit Iureconsultus in L. 13 § *Ex contrario*, de acquir: pot;, quibus praesupp: cujus textus est, quod in episcopatu universali retineatur a quolibet episcopo particulari

una pars in solidum, scil: cum alio et sic cum summo Pontifice, sed diversa ratione, quia ipse ratione plenitudinis potestatis, episcopus vero pro parte sollicitudinis, et ita sine difficultate ille textus interpretari potest, judicio meo. Ex quibus probatur, Summum Pontificem non habere nudum ministerium in concessione jurisdictionis, quam nobis communicat, non abdicando eam a Se. Cf. M. Bévenot, '*In Solidum* and St Cyprian', *Journal of Theological Studies* (N.S.), vol. v (1954), pp. 28 *seq.*; vi, 2 (1955), pp. 244 *seq.*

2 *Concilium Tridentinum*, tom. ix, p. 195, line 5, p. 210, line 1. Cyprian, *Ep.* lxvi.

3 *Ibid.* tom. ii, p. 735, line 5.

4 *Ibid.* p. 767, line 5.

5 *Ibid.* p. 824, line 28.

PAGE 50

1 *Ibid.* p. 851, line 22.

2 *Ibid.* p. 887, line 23: Ita expresse docet Cyprianus, ubi tria asserit; primo primatus Petro datur, secundo Christus in illis verbis: sicut me misit vivens Pater, etc: accipite spiritum sanctum etc: quibus recipiunt actualem missionem et cum spiritu sancto actualem omnem potestatem, tribuit actū apostolis omnibus parem potestatem actualem. *Nam hoc erant et caeteri apostoli quod fuit Petrus, pari consortio praediti et honoris et potestatis* actualis. Unde infert, quod sicut in apostolis, ita et in episcopis, apostolorum successoribus, *episcopatus unus est*, sicut missio apostolica et apostolatus, *cujus a singulis in solidum pars tenetur*, hoc est ad instar apostolorum. Quod curae et potestatis habet unus episcopus, alter obtinet in totam ecclesiam; nam hoc vult dicere in solidum, ut apud jurisconsultos plures fidejussores dicuntur aliquid promittere in solidum, quando unusquisque se rei totius fidejussorem constituit; ac adeo tota ecclesia, quae jure divino committitur in solidum cuivis episcopo, ad cuivis curam partialem spectat. Tertio extensio unius episcopatus in plures episcopos et ecclesiae

unius in plures ecclesias provenit ab uno episcopatu et una ecclesia, quae est supra singulos episcopos, qui omnes tenentur parere ecclesiae, quae *unum caput est et origo una et una mater foecunditatis...matrem.* Unde ecclesiam respectu singulorum apostolorum et episcoporum comparat corpori solis, trunco arboris, fonti: *avelle radium... latius expandit*: unum tamen caput et origo una et una mater ecclesia. Ubi Cyprianus refundit in ecclesiam tum apostolorum tum episcoporum jurisdictionis inaequalitatem, quam pro aristocratici sui tribunalis authoritate refert et ponit in singulis apostolis et episcopis prout in Domino videbitur expedire. Huic doctrinae Cypriani de aequalitate apostolorum omnes patres subscribunt.

3 *Ibid.* tom. IX, p. 222, line 48.

4 *Ibid.* p. 126, line 6: Apostoli a Christo immediate potestatem acceperunt, episcopi autem, qui in eorum locum successerunt, mediate per Papam....Ad id...quod unus sit episcopatus, respondit, ordinem et jurisdictionem duas partes formales episcopi esse, et de una Cyprianum locutum, sc: ordinis; alias si de jurisdictione intelligeret, destrueretur monarchia ecclesiastica. Nam cum dicit, quod a quolibet in solidum retinetur, necesse est ut de ordine intelligatur, in quo omnes sunt aequales.

5 *Ibid.* p. 129, line 5.

PAGE 51

1 *Ibid.* tom. II, p. 662.

2 S. Baluze, *Miscellanea* (ed. J. D. Mansi, 4 vols., Lucca, 1761–4), vol. III, p. 472; *Lettres, Anecdotes et Mémoires historiques du Nonce Visconti au Concile de Trente, par M. Aymon* (2 vols., Amsterdam, 1719), vol. II, pp. 79–83.

PAGE 52

1 Mansi, *Collectio Conciliorum*, tom. 16; *Concilii Vaticani*, 2, III, pp. 1031–2.

2 *Ibid.* p. 39, cp. *Epistola* LXXII, cap. 7; *ibid.* p. 61.

3 *Ibid.* p. 132.

4 *Ibid.* p. 167.

PAGE 53

1 *Ibid.* p. 184.

2 *Ibid.* p. 316.

3 *Ibid.* p. 453.

4 *Ibid.* pp. 109, 148.

5 *Ibid.* pp. 291–2.

PAGE 54

1 *Ibid.* pp. 372 *seq.*: Cyprianus...ait 'inde per temporum et successionem vices episcoporum ordinatio et ecclesiae ratio decurrit ut ecclesia super episcopos constituatur et omnis actus ecclesiae per eosdem praepositos gubernetur'. En interpretatio divi Cypriani in hunc textum; et tamen in schemate non citatur ut vult Cyprianus, non ut ecclesia super episcopos, sed super Petrum solum tanquam super petram fundamentalem constituatur....Quomodo igitur cum quattuor diversis interpretationibus SS. Patrum coram oculis, quarum una pene communis dici potest, illa scilicet Cypriani, Origenis et Chrysostomi; quarum alia antiquissima expressis verbis denegat sancto Petro idipsum quod in schemate asseritur, quomodo nunc in dogma fidei erigendum est et quidem vi hujus textus. Episcopatus enim, ut ait sanctus Cyprianus De Ecclesiae Unitate Lib. IV, unus est essentialiter, cujus in solidum pars tenetur; et hic episcopatus cum summo pontifice, de omnibus ad fidem spectantibus judicat et semper judicavit.

2 *Ibid.* pp. 393 *seq.*

PAGE 55

1 *Ibid.*: Sed sanctus Cyprianus in eodem textu et contextu dum praeclarissima haec de Petri primatu loquitur, loquitur una de juribus apostolorum et episcoporum, dicens iterato: Hoc erant utique et caeteri apostoli quod fuit Petrus, pari consortio praediti et honoris et potestatis; et

alias relate ad supremum pascendi munus docet, non solum Petrum sed omnes apostolos pariter esse pastores et totam per orbem ecclesiam unum gregem, ut unanimi omnium apostolorum consensione pascatur. Neque dicatur, ut mea saltem sententia minus recte hoc loco dictum est, hoc solum de apostolis praedicari, quasi episcopi non essent veri apostolorum successores, quasi non essent haeredes totius illius dignitatis et auctoritatis quae apostolis propria est, ut summus pontifex est verus successor beati Petri et verus haeres plenitudinis ejus potestatis quae sancto Petro propria est. Ideo sanctus Cyprianus continenter loquitur etiam de episcopis et dicit episcopatum in toto terrarum orbe unum et indivisum esse, cujus a singulis in solidum pars tenetur. Quae quidem sententia et doctrina sancti Cypriani docet ne illud, quod itidem hoc loco dictum est minus recte, quasi jurisdictio episcoporum ita ad limites dioecesis eorum restricta esset, ut nullo modo in reliquam ecclesiam pateat? Meo quidem judicio, praeter hanc jurisdictionem insita est vi characteris et ordinis episcopalis virtuale quoddam in reliquam ecclesiam jus.

2 *Ibid.* p. 457.

PAGE 56

1 *Ibid.* p. 502.

2 *Ibid.* p. 582.

3 *Ibid.* p. 609.

PAGE 57

1 *Ibid.* pp. 626 *seq.*: In quo praeclarissimo testimonio sanctus doctor quatuor veritates apertissime declarat; I. Quod promissio facta Petro fuit honor episcopatus et constitutionis ecclesiae expressio; II. Quod ex illa promissione originem habuit episcoporum successio; III. Quos ibi, nempe in episcopatu, sit constitutio ecclesiae; IV. Tandem quod ecclesia super episcopos, episcopi autem super Petrum constituti sint.

2 *Ibid.* p. 625.

3 *Ibid.* p. 810.

4 *Ibid.* pp. 771, 851, 867.

PAGE 58

1 *Ibid.* pp. 989, 1013, 1017, 1028–32.

2 *Pastor Aeternus*, cap. I.

PAGE 59

1 Cap. III.

2 Cap. IV.

3 Mansi, *op. cit.* pp. 29, 184.

PAGE 60

1 *Ibid.* pp. 194, 215.

2 *Ibid.* p. 318: Et novimus magnum illud testimonium sancti Irenaei, quod omnes nos contra Protestantes usurpamus. ...Bene notum est testimonium,...quisque vult perlegat dissertationem istam, quae est omnino ineluctabilis, non potest ei responderi...est compendium totius controversiae....Protestantes dicunt...*convenire* non significare *convenire in sententia*, *adhaerere in fide*; conveniunt, ut dicit Grabe Protestans, ut omnes pium iter faciant ad Romanam civitatem quia civitas Caesarum est.

3 *Ibid.* pp. 345–6: Testimonium vero solius Ecclesiae Romanae adfertur non solummodo quia est testimonium ecclesiae antiquissimae, sed quia est sufficiens et supremum; per traditionem enim et testimonium Ecclesiae Romanae omnes confunduntur haeretici....Ergo tandem judicia dogmatica summi Pontificis irreformabilia sunt per se, juxta doctrinam sancti Irenaei et sensum Schematis nostri....Quis non videt sanctum Irenaeum liquido et apertissimis verbis supremam authoritatem doctrinalem Romanorum Pontificium agnovisse et proclamasse?... Sic sanctus Irenaeus supremum Romanorum Pontificium magisterium seu infallibilitatem apertissimis verbis vindicat.

PAGE 61

1 *Ibid.* pp. 422, 523, 571.

2 *Ibid.* pp. 805 *seq.* (archbishop of Smyrna): Ad Irenaeum redeo. Omnes nostis ejus verba, quae pro Ecclesiae Romanae dignitate et auctoritate scripsit, et hic saepe citata....Et vero id necesse duplici de causa; altera propter potentiorem principalitatem seu primatum, quam prae caeteris obtinet; altera vero quia in ea semper conservata est, quae ab apostolis verae fidei et pietatis sincerae traditio. Immotum ergo restat ex Irenaeo de infallibilitate privilegium in summo Pontifice.

P. 836 (archbishop of Zara): Pontifex Romanus, inquam, prae primis et per excellentiam est testis et depositarius apostolicarum traditionum, juxta sanctum Irenaeum dicentem quod 'propter potiorem principalitatem necesse est omnem convenire ecclesiam', eo magis quod sola Romana Ecclesia est apostolicarum ecclesiarum superstes per non interruptam pontificium seriem.

P. 867 (bishop of Biella): Per apostolos constitutam esse ecclesiam et ita omnibus datum agnoscere quae vera videri debent et possint.

3 Lightfoot, *Apostolic Fathers*, part I, vol. I, p. 70.

PAGE 62

1 M. Bévenot, *St Cyprian's 'De Unitate'* (Bellarmine Series, IV, London, 1938); St Cyprian, *The Lapsed, the Unity of the Catholic Church* (Ancient Christian Writers, vol. 25, London, 1957).

PAGE 64

1 Mansi, *Collectio Conciliorum*, tom. 16; *Concilii Vaticani*, 2, III, pp. 81 *seq.*: Si ulla umquam papae epistola *ex cathedra* nuncupari poterit, haec est. Paulo post idem sanctissimus Papa ad Concilium IV Chalcedonense legatos misit, quibus publicationem illius suae epistolae iniunxit; inde sessione secunda concilii oecumenici IV epistola Leonis cum aliis documentis, praesertim cum quadam epistola Cyrilli Alexandrini perlecta est. Et quid inde? Cum patres

concilii epistolam Leonis plane consonam perspicerent cum antiqua fide et cum symbolis Nicaeno et Constantinopolitano, uno ore conclamarunt: 'Haec est fides patrum, omnes ita credimus. Petrus per Leonem ita loquutus est, pie et vere Leo docuit. Cyrillus ita docuit, Leo et Cyrillus similiter docuerunt.' Ergo patres concilii epistolam Leonis papae examini suo subjecerunt, an orthodoxa esset necne; et quia consonam eam iudicaverunt fidei antiquae, ideo eam approbaverunt. Si ipsis doctrina de infallibilitate pontificia cognita fuisset, epistolam Leonis nequaquam suo examini subiicere ausi forent; non de ea iudicassent, sex absque omni examine suppliciter et humiliter eam acceptassent. Deinde patres concilii IV pari modo epistolam Leonis et epistolam Cyrilli Alexandrini tractaverunt, pari modo eas habuerunt. Quid inde sequatur per se patet. Porro in sessione IV iuramento interposito, omnes episcopi interrogati sunt, num epistolam Leonis cum symbolis Nicaeno et Constantinopolitano conformem at consonam invenirent; ergo solemniter provocati sunt, de epistola Leonis et de eius orthodoxia iudicare. Quod si vere papam infallibilem putassent, plane alio modo agi debuisset. Non dictum est: ecce dogmaticam epistolam papae, audite et subiicite vos; sed dictum est, audite et iudicate. Sed non omnino omnes episcopi synodi IV epistolam Leonis plane orthodoxam habuerunt. Episcopi Illyrici et Palestinae tres locos huius epistolae haereseos suspectos putaverunt; et ideo in sessione secunda huic epistolae non consenserunt. Nemo dixit eis: quid agitis temerarii? non licet dubitare; plane non licet. Non ita dictum est. Plane alio modo cum eis actum est, et de iure ipsorum dubitandi nemo dubitavit.

PAGE 66

1 *Discours de Sa Sainteté Le Pape Pie XII* (7 Septembre 1955), p. 10; Merrill, *op. cit.* p. 332.

PAGE 68

1 H. E. Manning, *The Vatican Council and its Definitions*, pp. 68, 119.

PAGE 70

1 W. Chillingworth, *The Religion of Protestants*, CVI, pt. I, § 56, p. 290 (4th edition, London, 1674).

PAGE 71

1 G. H. Tavard, *Holy Writ or Holy Church* (London, 1959), p. 36. This study came to my notice after the delivery of these lectures but in time for me to take account of its interpretation in revising them for the press. I have found it most serviceable in the pre-Tridentine period; but the account of the Council of Trent and afterwards is the result of my independent investigation. Cp. also P. De Vooght, *Les Sources de la Doctrine Chrétienne d'après les Théologiens du XIVème Siècle et du Début du XVème* (Brussels, 1954). I am indebted to Dr T. M. Parker for these references.

PAGE 72

1 Luther, *Opera* (4 vols., Jena, 1556–8), vol. I. Disputatio J. Ecci et M. Lutheri Lipsiae habita, pp. 245 verso, 263 verso, 299 verso.

2 *Ibid.* vol. II (1557). *De Captivitate Babylonica*, p. 274 verso.

PAGE 73

1 *Ibid. Contra Regem Angliae:* Ita fit ut ego clamem: Evangelium, Evangelium, Christus, Christus: ipsi respondeant: Patres, Patres, usus, usus, Statuta, Statuta (p. 547 verso). Totus liber Henrici nititur hominum verbis et usu saeculorum, nullis Dei verbis, nec usu spiritus (p. 564 verso). Ego vero adversus dicta Patrum, hominum, angelorum, daemonum, pono non antiquum usum, non multitudinem hominum, sed unius majestatis aeternae verbum, Evangelium (p. 561 verso). Extra Scripturas nihil esse statuendum, aut si statuitur, liberum et non necessarium habendum (p. 562 recto).

2 'Bei Luther war die Heilige Schrift grundsächlich den Symbolen der altkirchlichen Tradition übergeordnet. Die Bibel allein war ihm kritischer Maßstab', F. W. Kantzenbach, *Das Ringen um die Einheit der Kirche im Jahrhundert*

der Reformation (Stuttgart, 1957), p. 103. I owe to Professor Gordon Rupp my introduction to this study.

PAGE 74

1 F. W. Kantzenbach, citing Melanchthon in *Corpus Reformatorum*, pp. 104, n. 2, 105, n. 8, 108, n. 24.

2 *Ibid.* p. 130, n. 24.

3 For Bucer, see Kantzenbach, pp. 124–41.

PAGE 75

1 H. Bullinger, *Decades*, vol. I, pp. 62, 64; vol. v, p. 533 (Parker Society).

PAGE 76

1 Tavard, *op. cit.* pp. 113, 118.

2 Tavard, *op. cit.* pp. 123–4.

PAGE 78

1 C. J. Hefele–H. LeClercq, *Histoire de Conciles*, tom. IX, part I, *Concile de Trente*, by P. Richard (Paris, 1930), pp. 252–8, 266–72. The text of the decree of the Council of Trent is: 'Sacrosancta...Tridentina Synodus...perspiciens hanc veritatem et disciplinam contineri in libris scriptis et sine scripto traditionibus, quae ab ipsius Christi ore ab Apostolis acceptae, aut ab ipsis Apostolis Spiritu Sancto dictante quasi per manus traditae ad nos usque pervenerunt...omnes libros tam Veteris quam Novi Testamenti, cum utriusque unus Deus sit auctor, necnon traditiones ipsas, tum ad fidem, tum ad mores pertinentes, tanquam vel oretenus a Christo, vel a Spiritu sancto dictatas et continua successione in Ecclesia catholica conservatas, pari pietatis affectu ac reverentia suscipit et veneratur.'

Text of decree as proposed on 22 March:... omnes Libros tam Veteris quam Novi Testamenti necnon traditiones ipsas tamquam vel oretenus a Christo vel Spiritu Sancto dictatas et continua successione in Ecclesia Catholica conservatas, quibus par pietatis debetur affectus, summa cum reverentia pro sacris et canonicis suscipit et veneratur, suscipique ab omnibus Christi fidelibus statuit et decrevit.

Concilium Tridentinum (ed. S. Merkle, Fribourg, 1911), vol. v.

Episcopus Fanensis: dixit: Cum jam receperimus Scripturas sacras, necessario recipiendae sunt traditiones, quae ab eodem Spiritu Sancto quo Scripturae datae sunt.

Ep. Bellicastrensis: a traditionibus, proposuitque recipiendas etiam esse traditiones Ecclesiae et ejus consuetudines, cum haec omnia principia sint nostrarum conclusionum.

Cardinal S. Croce: laudavitque, post sacros libros statim recipi traditiones; cum istae ab illis non differant nisi tantum, quod illi scripti sunt, hae non, sed ab eodem Spiritu et illos et istas descendisse; declaravitque, tria esse principia et fundamenta nostrae fidei; primum sacros libros, qui scripti sunt dictante Spiritu Sancto; secundum esse Evangelium, quod Christus Dominus Noster non scripsit, sed ore docuit et in cordibus illud plantavit, cuius Evangelii nonnulla postea evangelistae scripto mandarunt, multa quoque relicta sunt in cordibus hominum. Tertium, quia non semper Filius Dei corporaliter nobis mansurus est, misit Spiritum Sanctum qui in cordibus fidelium secreta Dei revelaret, et Ecclesiam quotidie et usque ad consummationem saeculi doceret omnem veritatem, et si quid in mentibus hominum dubii occurrisset, declararet (pp. 10–11).

Ep. Feltrensis: non censebat quod traditiones specialiter nominarentur, sed generaliter, cum difficile admodum esset, eas omnes nominatim recensere.

Card. Augustensis: A traditionibus; sed cum illae sint diversae auctoritatis in Ecclesia, diverso modo recipiendae sunt. Nam illae, quae ad fidem pertinent, eadem sunt recipiendae auctoritate qua recipitur evangelium, aliae autem non ita, cum earum plurimae immutatae fuerint, ut de bigamis, de esu, sanguinis et similia.

Card. Giennensis: ultra enim sacros libros nonnulla in Ecclesia Dei habemus, quae scripta non sunt, sed ipsius Ecclesiae auctoritate deservantur, cui Ecclesiae de apostolis tradita sunt et per manus ad nos usque devenerunt (p. 14).

EP. FANENSIS: inquiens, sibi videri iniquum, quod libri sacri et traditiones pari pietatis affectu reciperentur, cum inter haec maximum discrimen sit: Nam libri sacri immutabiles ac indelibiles sunt, traditiones vero et mutabiles et ab Ecclesia pro ejus arbitrio tolli possunt, ac etiam mutari....Praeterea cum sancta Synodus recipiat traditiones non scriptas, ut ex eis dogmata constituantur, de directo id pugnat assertioni Lutheranorum profitentium, nihil esse in Ecclesia recipiendum quod in sacris literis scriptum non reperiatur.

[The bishop suggested]: 'quoniam sancta haec Synodus scit, plura alia esse in Ecclesia a Spiritu Sancto dictata, quae in sacris literis non sunt prodita, propterea illa quoque suscipit et veneratur' (p. 40).

EP. VIGORNIENSIS: improbavit verba illa: *pari pietatis affectu*, inquiens: Et quis libros et traditiones ejusdem esse auctoritatis dicet? Nam traditiones observantur vel mutantur, vel omnino delentur, prout Ecclesiae una vel alia ratione, hoc vel illo tempore visum fuerit. At libros sacros quis umquam vel mutavit vel abolevit?

CONCLUSUM FUIT: ut capita dubitationum colligerentur et ad singulos Patres mitterentur et in futura congregatione per verbum *placet* vel *non placet* absolverentur (p. 41).

CAPITA: An satis sit, cum de traditionibus apostolorum fit mentio in decreto, agnoscere tales esse in Ecclesia, an vero per hoc decretum sit statuendum, eas esse et recipiendas esse. An placet dici, quod in decreto est scriptum...*quibus par debetur pietatis affectus*: an vero haec verba sint expungenda et alia illorum loco addenda, quae debitam utrisque reverentiam adhibendam exprimant.

An vero illis verbis suo loco manentibus, ille modus loquendi temperari debeat, addendo aliqua verba, quae hunc sensum exprimant, ut illis traditionibus, quae ad dogmata fidei pertinent, par pietatis affectus debeatur, qui illis dogmatibus quae in Scripturis exprimuntur.

Et eodem modo proportione in iis, quae ad mores pertinent, singula singulis referendo (p. 42).

A. Theiner, *Acta Genuina Concilii Tridentini* (2 vols., Zagreb, 1875), vol. 1.

EP. SENOGALLIENSIS: Non possum silere, quo dolo afficiar, dum video per decretum suscipi tantum traditiones quae usque ad nos pervenerunt, et propterea praetermissas, vel potius rejectas illas, quae ob Christianorum socordiam et negligentiam antiquitatae fuerunt, cum magis deceret in primis sanctum hoc concilium illas in lucem revocare (p. 84).

EP. CLODIENSIS: Non possum, inquit, pati, ut saepe dixi, Sanctam Synodum, *pari pietatis affectu* suscipere traditiones et libros sacros, hoc enim, ut vere dicam quod sentio, impium est.... Ut autem ego tantum deferam traditionibus, de quibus praesertim non sumus certi, quantum Evangelio, et quod eadem veneratione suscipiam traditionem illam apostolorum orandi versus orientem, ut Evangelium Joannis, impium mihi videtur (p. 85).

EP. CLODIENSIS dixit hoc verbum tantum: *obediam* (p. 89).

PAGE 88

1 Martin Chemnitz, *Examinis Concilii Tridentini Opus Integrum* (Frankfurt, 1596). De Traditionibus: Primum Genus Traditionum: Quod ea, quae Christus et Apostoli viva voce tradiderunt, quae postea ab Evangelistis et Apostolis literis consignata sunt, saepe vocantur traditiones (p. 61 *b*); Primum igitur genus Traditionum est quod Apostoli tradiderunt doctrinam viva voce, sed illa postea in Scripturae literis consignata est. Viri etiam apostolici multa annunciaverunt ab Apostolis accepta: sed σύμφωνα ταῖς γραφαῖς.

2 *Ibid.*: Secundum Genus Traditionum: Quod libri Scripturae sacrae non interrupta serie temporum...et certa connexionis successione, ab Ecclesia custoditi et fideliter ad posteros transmissi; nobisque quasi per manus traditi sunt.... Et hanc traditionem, qua nobis in manum dantur sacrae Scripturae libri, reverenter accipimus.... Ecclesia enim illa traditione fatetur, se alligatam esse ad

vocem doctrinae sonantis in Scriptura, et propagatione illius traditionis posteritatem etiam ad Scripturam alligatam esse docuit (pp. 62*b*–63*a*).

PAGE 89

1 *Tertium Genus*: Ita ergo ex traditionibus probant [Irenaeus and Tertullian] veritatem, authoritatem et sufficientiam Scripturae; quia scilicet eadem omnino sunt dogmata fidei, quae Scriptura continet, et quae primitiva Ecclesia, ex Apostolorum traditione accepta, usque ad illa tempora sincere custodierat. Nam ne apex quidem in tota illa Irenaei et Tertulliani disputatione ostendi potest de ullo dogmate, quod ex sola traditione ita producant, ut nullo Scripturae testimonio probari possit (p. 65*b*).

PAGE 90

1 *Quartum Genus*: Nullum enim est dubium primitivam Ecclesiam accepisse ab Apostolis et viris Apostolicis, non tantum textum (sicut loquimur) Scripturae, verum etiam legitimam et nativam ejus interpretationem, quam quia primitiva Ecclesia, ad illa usque tempora sine fictione custodierat, ita ut certis documentis probare posset, a quibus eam accepisset et ita retro progressus fieret ad ipsos usque Apostolos....Has vero germanas, antiquas et veras Apostolorum traditiones summa cum reverentia amplectimur (pp. 67*b*–68*a*).

2 *Quintum Genus*: illud, quod Patres aliquando ita vocant illa dogmata, quae non totidem literis et syllabis in Scriptura ponuntur, sed bona, certa, firma, et manifesta ratiocinatione ex perspicuis Scripturae testimoniis colligantur....Ad hoc quintum genus traditionum multae pertinent veterum disputationes de dogmatibus, quae reipsa in Scriptura, certa et firma habent testimonia, licet totidem literis et syllabis non exprimantur (pp. 68*b*–70*b*).

3 *Sextum Genus*: illud quod de Catholico Patrum consensu dicitur. Usitata enim est illa forma loquendi: Patres ita tradiderunt....Patrum enim scriptis suum et quidem honorificum, qui illis debetur, tribuimus locum....Est enim nostrorum sententia, quod in controversis religionis,

judex sit ipsum Verbum Dei, et quod postea accedat confessio verae Ecclesiae. Valet igitur in Ecclesia, sententia congruens cum Verbo Dei (p. 71*a*).

PAGE 91

1 *Septimum Genus*: quod ubi veteres mentionem faciunt Traditionum non Scripturam, proprie non intelligunt dogmata fidei sine Scriptura, extra et praeter Scripturam recipienda, etiamsi nullo Scripturae testimonio probari possent, sed de ritibus et consuetudinibus quibusdam vetustis loquuntur, quos propter antiquitatem ad Apostolos retulerunt (pp. 74*a*–*b*).

PAGE 94

1 *Octavum Genus*: de Traditionibus tam ad fidem quam ad mores pertinentibus, quae nullo Scripturae testimonio probari possunt, quas tamen pari reverentia et pietatis affectu Synodus Tridentina suscipiendas et venerandas imperat, sicut ipsam Scripturam. Num forsan Concilium intelligit tales traditiones, sicut veteres, quae in Scriptura continentur, et ejus perspicuis testimoniis probari possunt? Nihil vero minus. Petrus a Soto his verbis utitur: 'Infallibilis est regula et catholica; quaecumque credit, tenet et servat, Romana Ecclesia, et in Scriptura non habentur, illa ab Apostolis tradita.' Ut igitur locum hunc de traditionibus concludam, ostendimus nos non simpliciter omnes traditiones rejicere, quae hoc titulo et nomine apud veteres celebrantur. Quae enim aut in Scriptura continentur aut Scripturae consentaneae sunt, illas non improbamus. Sed de illis potissimum traditionibus quaestio est, quae (sicut Androdius inquit) nullo Scripturae testimonio probari possunt. In illis non sufficit simplex asseveratio, quod sit Apostolica traditio....Nec sufficit si ex Patribus aliquis dicat esse traditionem ab Apostolis profectam... (pp. 76*a*–*b*, 87*a*).

PAGE 95

1 Calvin, *Opera Selecta* (ed. P. Barth, 5 vols., Munich, 1926), vol. III, p. 14.

PAGE 96

1 *Institutio*, book I, cap. VII, § 1, p. 65; § 5, p. 70; cap, VIII, 12, p. 80.

PAGE 98

1 *Ibid.* book IV, cap. 8, § 8, pp. 139–40; § 9, p. 141; § 13, p. 146; § 14, p. 148; § 16, p. 150; cap. 9, § 8, p. 156; cap. 9, § 14, p. 162.

PAGE 99

1 *Ibid.* cap. 10, § 18; § 30, p. 192.

PAGE 102

1 R. Hooker, *Of the Laws of Ecclesiastical Polity*, I, xiv, 1, 2; II, viii, 7.

PAGE 103

1 *Ibid.* III, ix, 1; I, xiv, 5; V, lxv, 2.

2 Tavard, *op. cit.* pp. 242–3.

PAGE 104

1 Melchior Cano, *De Locis Theologicis* (Cologne, 1574), book III, cap. III, pp. 94v–99v.

2 Tavard, *op. cit.* p. 244.

PAGE 106

1 Flacius Illyricus, *Ecclesiastica Historia*, Praefatio.

2 Baronius, *Annales Ecclesiastici* (Antwerp, 1610), Praefatio: Satis superque puto, si germana illa ac sincera Ecclesiae vultus imago ex antiquo prototypo demonstretur....In hoc igitur nobis omni diligentia incumbendum, ut in primum illud exemplar semper mentis oculis intendentes, Ecclesiae effigies illa pristina pristino decori formaeque reddatur, quae suo splendore sic tenebras disjiciat, caliginemque dispellat, ut oculi intuentium maxima cum jucunditate clarissimo veritatis aspectu perfruantur... (p. 1).

Quamobrem res ipsas Ecclesiasticas Ecclesiastice pertractemus....Atque ut magis magisque eadem veritas elucescat, indiscussum nihil, quod ambiguum, vel veritati contrarium esse senserimus, uspiam relinquemus (p. 3).

Conabimur et in eo Thuycididen imitari, ut non tantum quid quolibet anno sit factum, sed et quid hieme, quid aestate, ac quid denique quibusque mensibus, cum licuerit, enarremus. Rem sane arduam et perdifficilem, ac nondum alicujus praevii ductoris calcatam vestigiis inimus viam....

Ad haec Catholicae Ecclesiae visibilem monarchiam a Christo Domino institutam, super Petrum fundatam, ac per eos legitimos verosque successores, Romanos nimirum Pontifices, inviolate conservatam, religiose custoditam, neque unquam interruptam vel intermissam, sed perpetuo continuatam; semperque hujus mystici corporis Christi, quod est Ecclesia, unum caput visibile; cui pareant membra caetera, esse cognitum et observatum per singula tempora demonstrabimus. Quibus porro incrementis Christiana Religio per totum se Orbem terrarum diffuderit, ac successione temporum longe lateque in unius visibilis capitis conjunctione coagmentata, atque in uno Spiritu fuerit propagata, aperiemus....

Haec itaque omnia et alia complura...sic pertractabimus, ut nihil dicamus leviter, aut inconsiderate, nihil inaniter, nihil quod non probatissimis testibus fulciatur, ratione demonstretur, probetur, conjecturis ac denique, quantum licet, perspicua solidaque veritate firmetur. Non enim doctas fabulas secuti sumus haec scribentes (dicamus confidenter) sed gravissimis usi testibus (pp. 4–5).

PAGE 109

1 Emanuel a Schelstrate, *De Disciplina Arcani: Dissertatio Apologetica* (Rome, 1685), *passim*, especially cap. I, IV, and VII.

PAGE 110

1 Tavard, *op. cit.* p. 149.

2 J. Jewel, *Works*, vol. IV, p. 889 (Parker Society).

3 Owen Chadwick, *From Bossuet to Newman*, p. 191.

PAGE 115

1 Tavard, *op. cit.* p. 36.

PAGE 119

1 A. Latreille, *L'Église Catholique et la Révolution Française* (2 vols., Paris, 1946–50), vol. 1, p. 83.

2 *Ibid.* p. 124.

PAGE 124

1 D. A. Binchy, *Church and State in Fascist Italy*, pp. 434–5.

PAGE 137

1 A. W. W. Dale, *Life of R. W. Dale* (London, 1899), pp. 268–9; cf. R. W. Dale, *History of English Congregationalism* (London, 1907), p. 659.

PAGE 139

1 A. W. Dale, *op. cit.* p. 275.

2 B. L. Manning, *The Protestant Dissenting Deputies* (ed. O. Greenwood, Cambridge, 1952), pp. 340, 353.

PAGE 140

1 M. Oakeshott, *The Social and Political Doctrines of Contemporary Europe* (Cambridge, 1939), pp. 156–7.

PAGE 141

1 *Ibid.* pp. 165–8, 178.

PAGE 142

1 *Ibid.* pp. 192–3, 196.

2 Binchy, *op. cit.* chs. xvi-xvii.

PAGE 145

1 S. Z. Ehler and J. B. Morrall, *Church and State throughout the Centuries: A Collection of Illustrative Documents* (London, 1954), p. 479.

PAGE 146

1 *Ibid.* pp. 491–2.

PAGE 147

1 *Ibid.* pp. 520–1.

PAGE 150

1 E. Ollivier, *L'Église et l'État au Concile du Vatican* (2 vols., Paris, 1877), vol. II, cap. VII.

PAGE 155

1 H. J. Laski, *Studies in the Problem of Sovereignty* (New Haven, 1917), pp. 112–13.

PAGE 158

1 Ehler and Morrall, *op. cit.* pp. 303–7; M. Oakeshott, *op. cit.* pp. 45–51.

PAGE 159

1 Binchy, *op. cit.* pp. 594–5.

PAGE 160

1 R. Aubert, 'Monseigneur Dupanloup et le Syllabus', *Revue d'Histoire Ecclésiastique*, vol. LI (1956), no. 1, pp. 79–142, nos. 2–3, pp. 471–512, no. 4, pp. 837–915; cf. L. Baunard, *Histoire du Cardinal Pie*, vol. II, pp. 218–19.

PAGE 162

1 Baunard, *op. cit.* (2 vols., Paris, 1887), vol. II, pp. 213–14.

2 Pro certo habentes, te, pro zelo, quo religionis et veritatis causam tueri soles, eo studiosius atque accuratius traditurum esse populo tuo germanam nostram literarum sententiam, quo vehementius calumniosas interpretationes iis affictas explosisti.

PAGE 163

1 Ehler and Morrall, *op. cit.* pp. 501–3, 598–9.

PAGE 164

1 Binchy, *op. cit.* p. 434.

NOTES

PAGE 165

1 J. H. Oldham, *Church, Community and State* (1933), pp. 17–18.

2 H. G. Wood, *Religious Liberty Today*, pp. 31, 89.

3 *Ibid.* p. 107.

PAGE 167

1 M. Creighton, *Persecution and Tolerance* (London, 1895), pp. 137, 139–40.

INDEX

Figures which follow a semi-colon refer to the Notes

INDEX